TRIBUTE
TO A
GENERATION

TRIBUTE
TO A

GENERATION

HAYDN WILLIAMS
AND THE BUILDING OF
THE WORLD WAR II
MEMORIAL

DAVID F. WINKLER

FOREWORD BY AMBASSADOR F. HAYDN WILLIAMS

NAVAL INSTITUTE PRESS
ANNAPOLIS, MARYLAND

Naval Institute Press
291 Wood Road
Annapolis, MD 21402

Library of Congress Cataloging-in-Publication Data

Names: Winkler, David F. (David Frank), date, author.
Title: Tribute to a generation : Haydn Williams and the building of the
    World War II Memorial / David F. Winkler ; foreword by Ambassador F.
    Haydn Williams.
Other titles: Haydn Williams and the building of the World War II Memorial
Description: Annapolis, Maryland : Naval Institute Press, [2020] | Includes
    index.
Identifiers: LCCN 2020021798 (print) | LCCN 2020021799 (ebook) | ISBN
    9781682475430 (hardcover) | ISBN 9781682475584 (pdf) | ISBN
    9781682475584 (epub)
Subjects: LCSH: World War II Memorial (Washington, D.C.)—History. | World
    War, 1939–1945—Monuments—Washington (D.C.) | Williams, F. Haydn,
    1919–2016. | War memorials—Washington (D.C.) | Mall, The (Washington,
    D.C.)—History.
Classification: LCC D836.W37 W56 2020 (print) | LCC D836.W37 (ebook) |
    DDC 940.54/65753—dc23
LC record available at https://lccn.loc.gov/2020021798
LC ebook record available at https://lccn.loc.gov/2020021799

This book would not be possible without the generous support and symbiotic partnership with the Friends of the National World War II Memorial, whose dedicated work of preserving the legacy of those who served in the world's greatest conflict ensures that their sacrifices will be forever remembered and revered.

IN MEMORY OF
F. HAYDN WILLIAMS

WE WERE MEMBERS of the Site and Design Committee for the National World War II Memorial. From 1994 to 2001 this committee was chaired by retired Ambassador F. Haydn Williams, resident of San Francisco and a commissioner of the American Battle Monuments Commission.

On more than one occasion, members of this committee referred to Haydn Williams as the "Father of the World War II Memorial." Without his leadership the Memorial would not be where it is nor would it have become the iconic representation, as now built, of the efforts of the World War II generation in the twentieth century.

Through many challenges, and sometimes disappointments, Haydn would often invoke the words of Daniel Burnham: "Think no small plans. They have no magic to stir men's blood." To have worked with him and witnessed his leadership and vision was a privilege to all who were involved in this endeavor.

On December 31, 2001, after our terms were over, Ambassador Williams sent a memorandum to Gen. P. X. Kelley (the new chairman of the American Battle Monuments Commission) titled rather mundanely: "Year End Report and Recommendations." Though the design of the World War II Memorial had been approved and the site secured, there were still some issues to be decided, including inscriptions. Williams, never one to leave a stone unturned, was still trying to put the final touches on this new Memorial.

The words inscribed today on the Announcement Stone on 17th Street are inspiring, yet they originated from a simpler, more powerful, and beautifully crafted two-sentence statement written by Williams. It alludes to his commitment to the site for the Memorial and to the subsequent work accomplished on what he deemed to be the crowning achievement of his personal and professional life. It also describes his vision for what he hoped the World War II Memorial would mean for future generations of Americans:

"UNITED IN A JUST AND COMMON CAUSE
HERE IN THE PRESENCE OF WASHINGTON AND LINCOLN
THE NATION HONORS ALL WHO SERVED THEIR COUNTRY
DURING THE SECOND WORLD WAR, THOSE IN UNIFORM,
THOSE WHO GAVE THEIR LIVES, AND ALL WHO SERVED ON THE
HOME FRONT. THIS MEMORIAL CELEBRATES THE GLORY OF
THEIR SPIRIT, THE BONDING OF THE NATION IN THE DEFENSE
OF FREEDOM, THE TRIUMPH OF LIGHT OVER DARKNESS,
AND THE QUEST FOR A JUST AND LASTING PEACE."

Members of the Site and Design Committee:
Brig. Gen. Evelyn "Pat" Foote, USA (Ret.)
Helen Fagin
Rolland Kidder
Frank Moore

February 20, 2020

CONTENTS

FOREWORD

T HE SELECTION of the site for the World War II Memorial and the development of its design is a long and involved story (as are the histories of the other great national monuments in Washington, D.C.). Here for the first time are the behind-the-scenes struggles and breakthroughs, told from the point of view of the "former Site and Design Committee (Old Working Group) of the American Battle Monuments Commission (ABMC)," which was created to oversee this major undertaking. The story focuses on the eight-year effort to find a site for the memorial, to select a designer through a national competition, and then to shepherd the process through several federal approving commissions. It is a personal narrative written with the passion of those who advocated and fought for the approval of the memorial's site and design.

The telling of this story through members of the ABMC's World War II Memorial Site and Design Committee has been encouraged by leading members of the American architectural community, by those engaged in the memorial's open national design competition, and by those who were intimately involved in the day-to-day process, including the designer, Friedrich St.Florian.

Over years of endless deliberations concerning location and design, and battling through open hearings, controversies, and delays, the committee was struck repeatedly by the fact that it was engaged in a singularly profound and historic experience. With the aforementioned encouragement, and after serious thought, the committee concluded that it has an obligation to share this unique experience by providing insights that the committee alone can provide. The resulting account will be a source for future historians, and at the same time will enhance public understanding of how the World War II Memorial came into being.

          Ambassador F. Haydn Williams
Chairman, World War II Memorial Committee (1994–2001)
San Francisco, California
March 2005

PREFACE

Now established as part of the central monumental core land-scape of the nation's capital, the World War II Memorial has become a magnet for veterans, tourists, and local residents to contemplate the service and sacrifice of what has been dubbed "The Greatest Generation." With three-quarters of a century having passed since the end of the global conflict, only a fraction of those who fought overseas and served on the home front during World War II remain to appreciate this national tribute, which was completed in time for the sixtieth anniversary of D-Day.

Fortunately, thanks in part to the efforts of hundreds of volunteers of a nonprofit organization known as the Honor Flight Network, some 200,000 who served had the opportunity to travel to Washington, D.C., during the fifteen-year window between the sixtieth and seventy-fifth anniversaries of the storming of the beaches at Normandy. There, they read the inscriptions and reflected on the stars positioned on the memorial's wall of honor, with each star representing one hundred of their comrades killed during the conflict. On many of these trips, the veterans and their volunteer handlers were welcomed by former senator Bob Dole, himself a veteran of World War II who had been wounded in that conflict.

The opening of the World War II Memorial served as an impetus for this program, which traces its roots to two thoughtful individuals—Earl Morse and Jeff Miller. Morse, who served as a physician's assistant at a Veterans

Administration clinic in Springfield, Ohio, got to know many of the patients under his care and drew inspiration from their stories. He welcomed the arrival of the new World War II Memorial as a national tribute to them. Recognizing that most of his patients lacked the means or ability to travel independently to the nation's capital, Morse, a former Air Force captain, offered to fly two of his patients to see the memorial. A member of an aero club, he convinced eleven of his fellow pilots to provide a similar service. On May 21, 2005, within a year of the opening of the memorial, six small aircraft arrived in D.C., carrying a dozen veterans and marking the first "Honor Flight."

Later that year Jeff Miller of Hendersonville, North Carolina, who had donated funds for the building of the World War II Memorial, saw what Morse had accomplished and initiated his own nonprofit HonorAir effort, which chartered commercial jets to bring larger groups to Washington, D.C. Morse and Miller met in 2007 and joined forces to form what is now known as the Honor Flight Network.

For the thousands of Honor Flight veterans, thousands of other veterans, the sons, daughters, grandchildren, and great-grandchildren of the Greatest Generation, and others who have made the trek to the Mall, the World War II Memorial melds well into the surroundings, flanked to the west by the magisterial Lincoln Memorial and to the east by the Capitol Building, which is partially blocked by the obelisk honoring the first president. Indeed, the architect Friedrich St.Florian considered the best compliment of his work to be when he overheard one visitor exclaim to another, "You mean this wasn't always here?"[1]

Given this current context of the World War II Memorial's tremendous popularity among the veterans and other visitors to the nation's capital, it's easy to forget that two decades ago the creation of this monument had become controversial. This is not the first effort to tell the story about the events preceding and following the American Battle Monuments Commission meeting of September 29, 1994. Christopher Shea published an article titled "The Brawl on the Mall" in the January/February 2001 issue of *Preservation* magazine. Three years later, Nicolaus Mills published the monograph *Their Last Battle: The Fight for the National World War II Memorial* in time for the structure's formal opening.

As we can infer from the titles of these publications, the siting and design of the World War II Memorial had detractors who coalesced to form a stiff opposition. In their narratives, both Shea and Mills placed the World War II Monument debate in context with the history of the National Mall. The mall was initially envisioned by Pierre L'Enfant and improved on by a commission convened by James McMillan, which brought together four of the nation's top urban planners at the dawn of the twentieth century—architects Daniel Burnham and Charles F. McKim, landscape architect Frederick Law Olmsted Jr., and sculptor Augustus Saint-Gaudens.[2]

The subsequent result of the McMillan Commission, the "Plan of 1901 for Washington," left a guiding template for future generations to follow regarding one of the nation's most significant public places. To ensure that the McMillan Commission's vision would not be tossed aside, Congress created a Commission of Fine Arts (CFA) in 1910 to advise on the location of fountains, statues, and monuments. Over time the CFA's mandate would grow, enabling it to have a greater say beyond the development of parks to include public buildings, structures adjacent to federal property, and buildings in historic Georgetown.

Under the guidance of the CFA, the federal government moved forward to implement the "Plan of 1901." One reason President John Quincy Adams had made a habit of bathing in the Potomac was that the river flowed much closer to the White House back then. That changed with the creation of the Tidal Basin in the 1880s, which would be ringed by Japanese cherry trees three decades later. Land directly west of the relatively recently completed Washington Monument was a swamp. The Plan of 1901 called for the swamp to be filled with a reflecting pool having not only an east-west axis but also a shorter north-south axis. At the far end of the pool, a monument for the sixteenth president was to be built. To the south, on an axis facing the White

House, another memorial would be built to honor the third president. The Plan of 1901 envisioned filling in the Tidal Basin and removing the Japanese cherry trees, to create a direct axis between the executive mansion and what would be the Jefferson Memorial. The removal of the Tidal Basin became one aspect of the Plan of 1901 that was never implemented. Another feature to create a north-south axis along the east-west Reflecting Pool was proposed but could not be built due to the construction of temporary government structures along the northern flank of the pool. These structures accommodated War and Navy Department staffing requirements during the Great War. When the Army vacated its Munitions Building spaces in 1943 for accommodations in the newly constructed Pentagon, the Navy filled the void. The "temporary" structures would serve the sea service until the late 1960s, with demolition occurring in 1970.

Following the dedication of the Lincoln Memorial in 1922, work was completed on the Lincoln Memorial Reflecting Pool, a third of a mile in length and 167 feet wide starting at the base of the memorial. While the Lincoln Pool was designed by Henry Bacon, a second adjacent pool was the creation of the aforementioned Olmsted and dedicated on October 15, 1924. Unlike Bacon's pool, the Olmsted pool featured 124 nozzles. As 124 streams of water shot into the air and turned to mist, the refracted light created perfect rainbows and hence, the pool earned its moniker "the Rainbow Pool."

As reflected in the title of Kirk Savage's 2009 monograph *Monument Wars: Washington's Transformational Landscape*, the World War II Memorial has been only one of the more recent objects of disagreement in the nation's capital, going back to the effort to memorialize the first president. Both Mills and Savage go into great detail to show there was no unanimity on any of the major monuments that awe us today within the core Mall area. Congressman Joseph Cannon had opposed the notion of building a monument to his hero Abraham Lincoln out in a swamp. Howls of protest from late-modernist architects savaged the proposal of classicist John Russell Pope to honor the third president. Though Pope's plans to replace the Tidal Basin with massive reflecting pools never came to fruition, the structure he designed, evocative of the Jefferson-designed library at the University of Virginia, was condemned as "a lamentable misfit in time and place."[3]

With the teardown of Navy buildings along the northern edge of the Reflecting Pool, the canvas for additional monuments opened up. A coalition of Vietnam veterans were able to lobby and gain approvals to build a memorial to honor those who had died in that conflict, where the former World War I vintage munitions building had stood. Opponents of the winning design by novice Maya Lin dubbed it the "black gash of shame." To ameliorate the opponents and also recognize those who fought and survived the war, a bronze sculpture of three soldiers in combat gear was placed facing the fold of Lin's "V" and a sculpture acknowledging the contribution of women was added later on. The Korean War Memorial, constructed across the way a decade later, was less controversial, but it also had its detractors.

Despite the initial opposition, the Vietnam Memorial was quickly embraced by veterans, their families, and others who had been affected by America's eleven-year involvement in Southeast Asia. Less than two decades removed from the conflict, many of those who visited were just coming into middle age and their memories had been repressed. Searching the wall and seeing the names of fallen comrades proved emotional and cathartic.

With one memorial completed and a national commitment to build a second one to honor the sacrifices made by American servicemen during the Korean War, the nation's lack of a memorial to honor those who served in uniform and on the home front during the war that preceded the Cold War seemed odd. In contrast with Korea and Vietnam, which had been regional conflicts in eastern Asia, John Keegan described World War II as "the largest single event in human history, fought across six of the world's seven continents and all of its oceans." Keegan, a noted British military historian, further observed that the war "killed fifty million human beings, left hundreds of millions of others wounded in mind or body and materially devastated much of the heartland of civilization."

Though a case can be made that World War II was initiated by Japan with its invasion of Manchuria in 1931, the consensus is that the conflict truly became a world war with the German invasion of Poland in September 1939, which led to declarations of war by both Great Britain and France. The conflict grew even more global in scope with the German invasion of the Soviet Union in June 1941, and finally with the air attack on the American naval base at Pearl Harbor from Japanese aircraft carriers six months later.

With the battle line of its Pacific Fleet smoldering at Oahu, the United States declared war on Japan on December 8, 1941, and on Germany and Italy a few days later. At the time of the United States' entry into the ongoing conflict, the momentum favored the enemy. Having carved up Poland with the help of the Soviet Union, Adolf Hitler turned west and north, capturing the Low Countries, driving around the Maginot Line to defeat France, then capturing Denmark and Norway. Able to evacuate its army at Dunkirk, Winston Churchill's Britain withstood an aerial bombardment starting in the summer of 1940 into 1941.

Unable to attain the needed air superiority to support a cross-channel conquest, Hitler's armies moved south to support Italian operations in the Balkans and North Africa before turning the brunt of their offensive power against the Soviet Union. At the time of the United States' entry into the war, Wehrmacht divisions had cut off the land approaches to Leningrad, stood on the outskirts of Moscow, and were moving to capture Stalingrad. Of immediate concern to the United States was a fleet of German U-boats that were then operating from France but would soon be operating off the U.S. eastern seaboard, in the Caribbean, and even in the Gulf of Mexico.

Meanwhile, with the blow delivered to American battleships at Pearl Harbor, Japan went on the offensive to secure oil reserves in what was known as the Dutch East Indies, invading the Philippines, occupying numerous western Pacific islands including Wake and Guam, and capturing the British crown colonies at Hong Kong and Singapore. As the calendar turned to 1942, with

Japanese naval forces operating in the Indian Ocean, Italian and German armies were poised to seize Egypt and conquer the Middle East.

Yet less than four years later, the war had been concluded with the total annihilation of the Axis powers. It was a multinational effort, with the Soviet Union and China by far making the greatest human sacrifice to ensure victory. However, it was the ability of the United States to not only mobilize, arm, and sustain its own forces but also support the armed forces of its allies that made the difference. World War II would prove to be the defining event of the twentieth century for the American people. Uniting the population to support one overriding cause, the war would help to break longstanding cultural norms regarding gender and race. And yet, decades after this monumental event, there was no national recognition of the service and sacrifice of the sixteen million who served in uniform and the tens of millions more who supported them on the home front.

Perhaps Ohio should dispense with its "Buckeye State" moniker in favor of "The Good Idea State," as the birthplace of aviation and home of the aforementioned Earl Morse was also the home of Roger Durbin. An Army veteran who fought in the Battle of the Bulge, Durbin attended a Lucas County township trustees meeting in February 1987 and shouted a question to visiting Congresswoman Marcy Kaptur: "How come there's no memorial to World War II in Washington?" The third-term representative from northwestern Ohio pondered for a second and said, "Well, there is—Iwo Jima." Wrong answer. Indeed, as Savage detailed in his critique of Washington monuments, "the work is often seen as a monument to the American triumph of World War II." But Savage affirmed what Durbin correctly pointed out to Kaptur: that the massive Felix de Weldon statuary abutting Arlington Cemetery was erected to honor the Marine Corps.[4]

To Kaptur's everlasting credit, she chose not to dismiss her constituent's query but looked into the matter and determined that Durbin's observation had been spot-on. Furthermore, having a seat on the House Veteran's Affairs Committee, she was positioned to act on it. On December 10, 1987, Kaptur introduced H.R. 3742, which proposed for the American Battle Monuments Commission to oversee the construction of a World War II memorial and museum on federal land in or near the nation's capital.

Despite bipartisan support and companion Senate legislation S. 2734, introduced by Senator Strom Thurmond of South Carolina, neither bill made it to the House or Senate floor for action by the end of the 100th Congress. During the 101st Congress, Kaptur introduced H.R. 537 and then H.R. 2807 when H.R. 537 ran out of steam. H.R. 2807 eventually made it through to the House floor, but the session ended before the bill could be called on for a vote. Senator Thurmond's new effort, S. 160, also fell flat. In addition, during the 101st Congress, Kaptur submitted H.R. 4365 for consideration. If it had been enacted, it would have directed the secretary of the treasury to mint a commemorative coin for sale, with proceeds supporting the memorial's construction. This resolution needed 218 cosponsors to vote for its passage on the floor, but it died in committee.

Following the start of the 102nd Congress, Kaptur, now in her fifth term, reintroduced the coin bill, now H.R. 1623, on March 22, 1990. At last, success! A year later, an amended version of the bill reached the floor and passed another year later on June 30, 1992. The Senate version S. 3195, championed by Senator John Glenn, a fellow Ohioan, passed at the end of September. With the two versions of the legislation ironed out in conference committee, on October 14, 1992, President George H. W. Bush signed Public Law 102-414, the World War II 50th Anniversary Commemorative Coins Act.[5]

Ironically, President Bush signed into law a funding mechanism for a memorial that had yet to be authorized. Parallel to the introduction of H.R. 1623 came H.R. 1624—Kaptur's latest version of the memorial legislation. Passed in the House a week before the coin bill, Kaptur and her colleagues awaited action in the Senate, where Senator Thurmond's S. 2244 passed at the end of September. One hiccup though: Senator Thurmond had called for a nonprofit organization, the National World War II Memorial Fund, to be the builder. When the two pieces of legislation went to conference committee, the version that emerged retained Kaptur's provision that the memorial be built under the auspices of the ABMC. The Senate voted for the amended legislation on October 7 and sent it back to the House for final approval. However, anxious to adjourn to campaign during a presidential election year, the House began its recess without action, killing H.R. 1624.

By now, the effort to gain legislative support to authorize and build the memorial had taken longer than America's involvement in World War II. Reelected to a sixth term, Kaptur introduced H.R. 682 on January 27, 1993. A day earlier, Thurmond introduced S. 214. This time, the bureaucratic process in the 103rd Congress proved more supportive. On May 25, 1993, with Senator Thurmond, Congresswoman Kaptur, and Roger Durbin looking on, President Bill Clinton signed Public Law 103-32 into law.[6] The 103rd Congress also needed to respond to a provision of the 1986 Commemorative Works Act stating that any commemorative work in a zone defined as Area I (the vicinity of the National Mall) needed congressional approval. On October 6 and 7, 1994, the House and Senate passed Joint Resolution 227, authorizing the placement of two new monuments in the capital's core area—the Thomas Paine Memorial and the World War II Memorial. The resolution would be signed into law by President Clinton on October 25. Unlike the World War II Memorial, which required a compromise between the Senate and the House to place it under the auspices of the ABMC, responsibility for the Paine tribute was awarded to the nonprofit Thomas Paine National Historical Association. The Paine Memorial has not been built.

ACKNOWLEDGMENTS

THE FOREWORD by Ambassador F. Haydn Williams was meant for a book intended for publication well over a decade ago, which was to detail the challenges faced by what was first called the Site and Design Committee, then the World War II Memorial Committee, and finally (after a change in presidential administrations) the Old Working Group, in their efforts to find a location, select a winning design, redesign that winning design, and then persevere to incorporate the details that led to the final drawings of what has become one of the nation's more substantial commemorative complexes—the World War II Memorial.

That book had been intended as a collaborative effort between those who had served on the committee that had been initially established in late 1994 by the chairman of the American Battle Monuments Commission, Gen. Frederick F. Woerner Jr., USA (Ret.). Woerner had just been given the responsibility, thanks to congressional legislation, of siting and building a memorial aimed at honoring those who had served the nation during World War II. The purpose of the Site and Design Committee, which had initially been led by the former governor of New York, Hugh Carey, is fairly self-explanatory. With the departure of Governor Carey as a commissioner with the ABMC, the burden of leadership fell to Ambassador Williams, who eagerly seized the reins. More famous names would become associated with the campaign to construct a complex that would memorialize the approximately 404,800 Americans who made the ultimate sacrifice for their country, and to honor the millions more who fought overseas or worked on the home front to achieve a common objective. Senator Bob Dole and FedEx chairman Fred Smith served as the cochairs of the capital campaign, and Tom Hanks became the public face of an effort that successfully appealed to multiple generations.

However, the eventual site and shape of the complex currently located on the Mall west of the Washington Monument would be far different had it not been for the involvement of Williams. At the beginning of the site selection process, the Rainbow Pool site of the current memorial wasn't even offered for consideration. Following his "Eureka!" moment, Williams skillfully persuaded a bureaucracy of planning commissions and federal agencies to agree upon a location, which President Clinton would consecrate with soil from America's overseas cemeteries on Veterans Day in 1995. Williams was aided in this effort by a small team of exceptional individuals from diverse backgrounds who were assigned to his committee, along with some potent allies such as the chairman of the Commission of Fine Arts, J. Carter Brown. Each of these individuals played a significant role in working with the design architect, Friedrich St.Florian, to create what we have today. Each of them also displayed a spirited willingness to confront critics of the project.

Living in the nation's capital is both a blessing and a curse. The blessing is that the District of Columbia hosts some of the world's greatest cultural and intellectual resources within the halls of its museums, libraries, and archives. The economy is recession-proof given that government will never go out of business. However, visiting tourists do take note of D.C.'s license tags, which state "Taxation Without Representation." No senators represent the District, although it has a population greater than each of the states of Vermont and Wyoming. The District does have a representative in the House, but Eleanor Holmes Norton, the representative at the time of this writing, has no voting authority. Though the citizens of the District have been able to vote for their own mayor and district council since 1975, Congress retains the prerogative to review and overturn council-generated legislation. With some issues, such as gun control, some in Congress have not hesitated to impose their nonurban values and beliefs on the local population.

Add to this constitutionally imposed friction, there is a continuous desire from groups in the hinterland to commemorate/celebrate/memorialize certain individuals/institutions/organizations and historical events in the nation's capital with markers, statues, or other significant architectural displays. No other American city is shaped by outside influences the way Washington, D.C., is. Meanwhile, some of those living in the District, who are the benefactors of all of this national largesse, may have preferred alternative uses of the local public space. Unlike other cities where the city council has tremendous sway on what gets built where, in the nation's capital, Congress and several commissions, composed mostly of appointees from the president, federal agencies, and local governments, are the arbiters.

The question asked by Ohioan and World War II veteran Roger Durbin to his Congresswoman Marcy Kaptur on why there had been no World War II Memorial built in the nation's capital would eventually lead to this underlying friction boiling over publicly. In pushing through their desire to build the memorial on the National Mall at the Rainbow Pool site, and following the ensuing design selection process, the ABMC provoked a reaction within local civic organizations leading to the creation of a "National Coalition to Save Our Mall" counter-campaign organization.

The locally based opposition would have an impact on the ultimate design of the World War II Memorial, as criticism scuttled much of the first proposed design and influenced the redesign of the memorial we view today. However, with the opposition's ultimate goal of having the memorial built at another location, the issue seemed to be heading to the courts for ultimate arbitration until Congress stepped in to pass legislation dictating that the memorial would be built and prevent further legal recourses blocking construction. Though defeated, those who mobilized to preserve the Mall without a World War II memorial gained from the experience and morphed themselves into the National Mall Coalition, a nonprofit organization that is dedicated to visionary planning for the National Mall as it enters into its third century at the heart of the nation's capital. A major focus of the group has been ensuring that maintenance of the memorials, monuments, and surrounding vegetation is adequately funded. Given this new mission, there are now shared interests between the former opposition and those who waged the successful campaign to build the World War II Memorial.

Ironically, had Ambassador Williams published his collaborative book recounting the siting and design of the memorial back at the time of its dedication, the story would have had an unfinished ending. Returning to the memorial a year after the 2004 grand dedication, Williams noted that the structure and grounds were not being properly maintained—worse, that the memorial was not living up to its potential as a focal point for commemoration and public education concerning the most climactic event of the twentieth century. Colleague Helen Fagin looked over at the disappointed ambassador, who expressed his anguish and concluded, "This is unacceptable!"

Thus, Williams led the effort to create a nonprofit organization, the Friends of the World War II Memorial, to support commemoration efforts and develop strong educational outreach programs. Williams served as the organization's first chairman, recruited its initial board of directors (several of whom are still serving), and helped raise funds to support the activities associated with this unique Washington landmark. And with his passing in 2016, he bequeathed the Friends of the World War II Memorial additional funds to support new initiatives (such as the telling of this story!).

I am appreciative to the current chair of the Friends organization, Josiah "Si" Bunting III, for entrusting me to write the narrative of the siting and design of the memorial. As for contributing material for the narrative, Ambassador Williams deserves the greatest accolades for his years of generating memoranda, detailed record keeping, and organizing those papers into some forty-four Hollinger boxes that are retained at the National Defense University (NDU). Also at NDU are Helen Fagin's papers. At the NDU I thank Susan Lemke and Abigail Gardner for making those records accessible. Next are the surviving members of the Site and Design Committee, later known as the Old Working Group: Rolly Kidder, Helen Fagin, Pat Foote, and Frank Moore, who contributed their own insights on the site and design process. Kidder deserves an extra shout-out for taking a trip to Providence, Rhode Island, to research the J. Carter Brown Papers at Brown University in support of this project.

Other key individuals involved with the project who contributed to this narrative include the former ABMC chair Gen. Fred Woerner, the former ABMC secretary Maj. Gen. John Herrling, project officer Col. Kevin Kelley, sculptor Ray Kaskey, public relations director Mike Conley, and architect Friedrich St.Florian. In getting the perspective from the Hill, I thank former Senator John W. Warner. As I finish this narrative, I am also editing an oral history we collaborated on with the senator for publication with the U.S. Naval Institute. I also credit Nicolaus Mills and Thomas Grooms, who authored the General Services Administration narrative of the project, for laying the foundation for this narrative with their respective books of the memorial published at the time of its dedication. Whereas this book benefited from newly archived materials, Mills and Grooms were able to connect with a larger number of individuals who were working on the project at the time. This narrative is enriched thanks to their earlier diligence.

The Friends of the National World War II Memorial is a dynamic organization that has made the memorial a focal point for telling the story of the Greatest Generation through a robust on-site volunteer program, sponsored talks (including the annual F. Haydn Williams Lecture at National Defense University), and teacher workshop programs. Executive Director Holly Rotondi is the hidden hand behind the organization's vibrancy and could not have been more supportive. I appreciate her connecting me with key individuals involved in the building of the memorial, and her creation of a book review committee to correct any misinterpretations I had of the documentary materials. The members of the committee were: Friends Chairman Si Bunting; Vice Chair Jane Droppa; Vice Adm. Jack Baldwin, USN (Ret.); Rear Adm. John Bitoff, USN (Ret.); Bob Bohannon; Brig. Gen. Evelyn "Pat" Foote, USA

(Ret.); Rolly Kidder; Frank Moore; Bob Peck; Ruth Rodgers; Holly Rotondi; and Thalia Ertman.

In addition, because several on the committee couldn't resist the temptation to correct typos and grammar, my friends at the Naval Institute Press—Rick Russell, Tom Cutler, and Jim Dolbow—received a much cleaner narrative from me to work with than they have in the past! I thank copy editor Jehanne Moharram, who made additional edits to get this book to press.

Of course, throughout this project, my wife Mary and daughters Katherine and Carolyn have been most supportive. Love ya!

David F. Winkler
Alexandria, Virginia
February 2020

Abbreviations

ABMC	American Battle Monuments Commission
ACHP	Advisory Council on Historic Preservation
ATF	alcohol, tobacco, and firearms (not the "Bureau of")
CFA	Commission of Fine Arts
CIA	Central Intelligence Agency
CPFC	Campaign Policy and Fundraising Committee
ESI	Edwin Schlossberg Incorporated
GSA	General Services Administration
MAB	Memorial Advisory Board
NATS	Naval Air Transport Service
NCMC	National Capital Memorial Commission
NCPC	National Capital Planning Commission
NDU	National Defense University
NPS	National Park Service
NROTC	Naval Reserve Officers Training Corps
POW	prisoner of war
PSA	public service announcement
SDC	Site and Design Committee
VFW	Veterans of Foreign Wars

Chapter One

ENTER F. HAYDN WILLIAMS

ADM. WILLIAM J. CROWE served as the chairman of the Joint Chiefs of Staff during crucial periods of the presidencies of both Ronald Reagan and George H. W. Bush, as the Soviet Empire imploded and conflict raged in the Middle East between Iraq and Iran. With a PhD from Princeton and a strong background in political-military affairs, the Oklahoman had earned the trust of the two presidents and the secretaries of defense under whom he had served. However, Crowe's path to the top uniformed position in the U.S. military was hardly preordained. Graduating from the U.S. Naval Academy after World War II, Crowe chose submarines as a career path and rose to command *Trout*, a diesel boat that had been built after the end of World War II. Following his tour in *Trout*, his career took an unconventional turn when he was accepted at Princeton to pursue both a master's degree and a doctorate in political science. In doing so he declined an opportunity to enter the Navy's nuclear power program. In an interview with Adm. Hyman G. Rickover following his first year at Princeton, Crowe explained that he would be happy to enter the program upon receiving his degree. Rickover would not hear of it.[1] With the Navy's submarine force rapidly turning to nuclear power for propulsion, there seemed no long-term future for Crowe in the undersea realm. Instead, the Navy assigned him to political-military billets predominantly in the Pacific. He documented those various assignments in his 1993 book *In the Line of Fire: From Washington to the Gulf—the Politics and Battles of the New Military.*

Following a three-year stint as the head of the East Asia and Pacific Branch within the office of the Chief of Naval Operations in the Pentagon, Crowe served with U.S. naval forces in South Vietnam under the command of Vice Adm. Elmo R. Zumwalt Jr. However, Crowe's hopes for a major follow-on afloat command—a ticket that needed to be punched if he were to have any shot at flag officer rank—seemed dashed when he received a call from Washington with the opening query, "Did you ever hear of Micronesia?" Then Crowe, now a captain, was informed about the forthcoming Micronesian Status Negotiations and that his name came up as a potential Navy representative in discussions with the current Chief of Naval Operations, Adm. Thomas Moorer. "Well, I don't want to go," Crowe responded. He would not have much choice in the matter. Both Moorer and Zumwalt agreed that Crowe would be the perfect naval representative to the newly created Office of Micronesian Status Negotiations within the Department of the Interior. There he would report to F. Haydn Williams.[2]

Crowe had no idea who Williams was, but he would soon learn. Haydn Williams was the son of Welsh immigrants, born on August 29, 1919, at Spokane, Washington. Crowe recalled that Williams' father was a Presbyterian minister who subsequently moved to Oakland, California. Thus, young Haydn and his three older sisters were raised in a household that valued discipline, godliness, and academic excellence. The *San Francisco Examiner* later quoted Williams saying, "Since childhood my life has been guided by the hymn 'Work, for the Night is Coming.'"[3]

Accepted at the University of California at Berkeley, Williams successfully completed some college coursework. However, to raise additional tuition, he signed on with Pan American Airlines, which was contracted to help construct facilities on Midway Island. On the morning of December 7, 1941,

Williams was playing touch football with some of his fellow workers when two Japanese destroyers appeared offshore and started shelling the naval installation. The young men scrambled for cover as Marine Corps artillery shot back and scored a hit on one of the ships, now those of an enemy. However, the Japanese gunfire would claim the lives of four servicemen and injure one of Williams' coworkers named Roy—permanently paralyzing him. Thinking that the bombardment was a prelude to an invasion, Williams took his personal papers and diaries and buried them. Evacuated from Midway, Williams eventually did return, only to find that a runway had been built over his burial spot.[4]

Unlike many of his peers, Williams did not run to a recruiting station as soon as he learned of the devastation wrought by the Japanese air attack conducted on Pearl Harbor, Hawaii, one thousand miles to the southeast. He was under contract for Pan Am, and the Navy contracted Pan Am to provide essential services ranging from air terminal management and aircraft repair to air transport services, food preparation, and aircraft ferrying. Over the next two and a half years, Williams became adept at various aspects of air traffic control, and Pan Am designated him as an airport manager. Posted at the Naval Training and Distribution Center at Treasure Island in the middle of San Francisco Bay, Williams likely made several trips out to Hawaii to assist with Transport Squadron TEN (VR-10), the Naval Air Transport Service (NATS) squadron that handled aircraft maintenance and operations for the Navy's growing fleet of cargo planes. As civilian contractors, Pan Am employees were to stay clear of the war zone. However, in the event Pan Am people were needed for the western Pacific, there was a contingency made to bring them on to active duty. For this contingency, Williams was enlisted on October 17, 1942, but continued to work as a civilian. As his work responsibilities increased commensurate with his Navy active-duty counterparts, Williams was commissioned an ensign on December 8, 1943. However, he remained in civilian status, given his critical work for Pan Am. That changed in mid-1944 as VR-10 had grown to more than seven thousand personnel and had become unwieldy in attempting to perform maintenance and handle flight operations. Thus VR-12 was commissioned as a squadron responsible for flight operations for a naval air network, which stretched nearly 21,000 nautical miles. To create VR-12, NATS reassigned a number of VR-10 personnel and militarized several hundred Pan Am employees. On July 17, Ensign Williams came on active duty.[5]

Williams joined VR-12 when it was initially based at Naval Air Station Honolulu. He was then sent with a detachment to Johnston Island, arriving there on October 22, 1944. Centrally located some 750 nautical miles southwest of Hawaii, Johnston Island served as a hub for aircraft flying to the southwestern and western Pacific island chains. The VR-12 unit history described the air station as the busiest in the world for its size. Williams was designated as an air transport officer. Monthly squadron musters had him there until the spring, after which he performed the same duties on Guam. Later, well after the Battle of Leyte Gulf, Williams reported to VR-10, which had established a maintenance facility on the island of Samar in the Philippines. Arriving at these locations after the fighting had ceased, Williams repeatedly saw the remnants of the carnage where thousands of Americans had paid the ultimate price to capture the islands of Saipan, Tinian, and Guam. Their sacrifices were not in vain and certainly would never be forgotten by Williams, who had handled the scheduling of flights to and from forward airbases that now brought Japan within striking distance of newly arriving B-29 bombers. Eventually, those forward bases at Saipan and Tinian served as the launch point for the *Enola Gay* and *Bockscar*, the aircraft that dropped atomic weapons on, respectively, Hiroshima on August 6, 1945, and three days later on Nagasaki.[6]

At the end of August, Williams was one of the first victorious Americans to arrive in Japan, ultimately landing at the Japanese naval air station at Kisarazu across Tokyo Bay from Yokohama. From that vantage point, he would have undoubtedly witnessed the arrival of the vast armada of the U.S. Pacific Fleet, as well as the flyover of hundreds of American warplanes that arrived for the surrender ceremonies on *Missouri* on September 2, 1945. However, Williams probably did not dwell much on the significant events occurring out on the bay, since he had the meaningful duty of locating prison camps and organizing the repatriation of American prisoners of war (POWs). Involved in all aspects of the mission, he even lent a hand in cooking big pots of stew for the malnourished captives. One of the POWs he encountered was Maj. Gregory "Pappy" Boyington, a Marine aviator who had "posthumously" received the Medal of Honor after he had been shot down and presumed lost over Rabaul. A grateful Boyington presented Williams with a bugle he had collected from the camp in which he had been held.[7]

Released from active duty in early 1946, Williams completed his academic course work to attain his bachelor's degree from Cal Berkeley later that year and the promising scholar immediately was accepted to attend the Fletcher School's graduate program of international studies at Tufts University. He obtained his master's degree in 1947. An MA enabled him to return to the state of his birth to teach at the University of Washington. In 1954, Williams returned to Tufts, appointed as the associate dean and an associate professor at the Fletcher School. In his spare time as he worked on his dissertation for his doctorate, titled *A Study in British American Civil Aviation Relations—The Opening of the Atlantic and Pacific Airways*, which was completed in 1957. Following the defense of his dissertation and receiving his doctorate, Williams earned an appointment as the deputy secretary of defense for international security affairs, to work in the Pentagon under John "Jack" N. Irwin II. Such was the close friendship between Irwin and Williams that Irwin's young children took to calling the deputy secretary "Uncle Haydn."

Within the E-Ring of the Pentagon, Williams' attention to detail and ability as a taskmaster earned him the nickname "Bulldog." President Dwight Eisenhower didn't care for a large cadre of staffers at National Security Council meetings. So limited, Secretary of Defense Thomas Gates chose Williams to tag along to take notes of the proceedings. He remained in that post into the Kennedy administration, noting the total change of atmosphere of the NSC meetings from the business-like, one-hour Eisenhower-run meetings to the more collegial clubhouse Kennedy style. Though the new president may have lightened things up at the White House, the new secretary of defense,

Robert McNamara, was a different matter. McNamara kept Williams busy during the first year of the Kennedy administration, tasking him with serving as a member of the fourteen-nation conference on Laos, assigning him to assist the secretary of state at the Organization of American States Conference, and designating him to participate in the President's Special Committee on International Civil Aviation Policy.[8]

Despite being a rising star in the Pentagon bureaucracy, Williams decided to toss his government career path aside in 1962 for academia and departed to the University of Washington at Seattle. Likely a bride and a son played a factor in this sudden career shift. Williams had married the former Margaret French, who had a son, Thomas, from a previous marriage.

Six months his senior, Margaret was a Hickman, Kentucky, native who eventually earned a college degree at the University of Tennessee. Whereas Haydn had served as a contractor for Pan Am at the onset of the war and later earned a Navy commission to serve with the Naval Air Transport Service, Margaret worked for American Airlines, which was contracted by the Army Air Transport Service to provide aircraft to support the service's logistical needs. At the conclusion of World War II, American Airlines offered her an opportunity to work in the corporation's Government and Congressional Relations Office, where she roamed the halls on Capitol Hill to meet legislators who had oversight on air transportation matters, as well as meeting administration officials at the other end of Pennsylvania Avenue. The five-foot-seven brunette exuded glamour and enjoyed conversation. Given Haydn's service background and eventual dissertation topic, it's hard to imagine the two lacked for discussion material when they eventually met. Haydn was smitten with her charm and ability to make him laugh. Margaret admired his intellect. After a relatively short courtship, the two married in 1960.[9]

While in Seattle, Haydn and Margaret often hosted another couple. Lt. Jack Baldwin, detailed to the Naval Reserve Officers Training Corps (NROTC) unit at the University of Washington as part of the Navy's graduate oceanography program, was told by his sister-in-law to look up her half-sister, who was married to a member of the faculty. Jack and Haydn's ensuing friendship would prove to be a relationship that not only endured socially, but professionally as well. Baldwin would eventually retire as a vice admiral, having served as the president of National Defense University on whose Board of Visitors a much more elderly Haydn Williams sat.

In 1964, the Williams family relocated to San Francisco, where Williams had been appointed president of the Asia Foundation. This was an organization that had been founded a decade earlier by a consortium of corporate and academic leaders as a nonprofit, nongovernmental organization that would work to develop democratic institutions in the war-torn and developing nations of Asia and the Western Pacific. That was the cover story. A report prepared for the U.S. Senate Committee on Foreign Relations in 1983 traced the roots of the organization "to the establishment of an ostensibly private body, 'the Committee for Free Asia' in 1951, sanctioned by President [Harry] Truman's National Security Council and with the knowledge of Congressional Oversight Committees." In 1954, the committee rebranded itself as the Asia Foundation and incorporated in California as a nonprofit. Given the establishment of Communist regimes in China, North Korea, and North Vietnam, the thinking in the Eisenhower administration was that a privately governed nonprofit "would have the freedom and flexibility to do things the government would like to see done which it chose not to do or could not do directly as well."[10]

Thus, the Asia Foundation benefited from direct Central Intelligence Agency (CIA) covert funding or indirect funding through other entities that received CIA support. Aware that the media was making inquiries and would eventually break a story regarding the foundation's funding, the CIA issued a preemptive news release in March 1967, announcing that it had provided funds for the San Francisco-based nonprofit but minimizing the extent of the support. Not surprisingly, the announcement undermined the legitimacy of the Williams-led organization overseas. Consequences included the eviction of foundation representatives from India. With the cat out of the bag, President Lyndon B. Johnson directed that covert CIA funding be terminated. Jan Evans

Houser recalled that her first husband, Ben Evans, who worked at the agency's headquarters at Langley, was provided with a briefcase stuffed with $1 million and told to fly out to San Francisco, hand it off to Haydn, and wish him luck. President Johnson did establish a commission, led by Secretary of State Dean Rusk, to review the fate of the organization. The commission concluded that the Asia Foundation served the national interest and was worthy of overt federal funding. In later years the U.S. Agency for International Development and the State Department's Bureau of Educational and Cultural Affairs would funnel millions in grants to support Asia Foundation initiatives.

The viability of the Asia Foundation would be reexamined during the Nixon and Ford administrations, both concluding that the organization's educational programs and work to foster relationships with future overseas leaders were in line with national foreign policy objectives. In 1979, the Office of Management and Budget directed that the State Department should continue on as the source for Asia Foundation federal funding. Meanwhile, Williams made strides to diversify his organization's funding streams, partnering with the Henry Luce Foundation in 1974 to administer the Luce Scholars Program, which offered opportunities for American college seniors, graduate students, and young professionals to travel and work professionally in Asian countries. Nominated by some seventy-five of the nation's leading colleges and universities, ideal candidates demonstrate leadership abilities and show the promise of advancing far in their chosen career paths.[11] Margaret embraced this initiative, hosting a send-off reception for the fifteen to eighteen scholars selected per annum and keeping in touch with the young men and women during their time overseas and after their return. Though Haydn was president of the Asia Foundation, it really was a package deal, because Mrs. Williams traveled extensively throughout Asia to advance the organization's objectives. One of her more memorable experiences was traveling to Beijing in 1980 to open the Asia Foundation's office in that Communist nation.[12] Among the locations she had previously visited were the islands of Micronesia.

On the morning of March 11, 1971, Haydn Williams received a surprise call from Howard Levin, who served on Henry Kissinger's National Security Council staff. Levin informed Williams that his former Pentagon boss, who now served as the undersecretary of state in the Nixon administration, had placed Williams on a short list for consideration to lead negotiations on the future status of Micronesia. A week later, Haydn was in Washington.[13]

When Captain Crowe arrived to serve under Williams, he discovered that the disputes lay not between the Micronesians and Washington but between the State Department, which favored severing ties, and the Defense Department, which favored retaining links for basing rights. Crowe noted that, though Williams was appointed as an ambassador, certain State Department personnel viewed him as an amateur and a figurehead who should defer to their views. "Well, Haydn didn't agree with that at all."[14]

Crowe had some familiarity with the region, having traveled through Saipan and Guam. Over the next few months, he traveled extensively to the different island groups, learning about the different cultures, languages, topographies, and economies. Finally, after the negotiating team had developed an appreciation of the issues they would confront, the first set of talks were held in Washington with representatives from the various island groups. Given the sightseeing and entertainment opportunities presented in the nation's capital, Crowe recalled they had to send out search parties to get them back to the negotiating table. After that unproductive series of talks, "Haydn gave some thought to that and the next set of negotiations were in Hana, Maui."

Though in a tropical paradise, Hana was on the eastern tip of the Hawaiian resort island, with a claim to fame of being close to the burial site for Charles Lindbergh and his wife in nearby Kipahulu and only being accessible by either a long winding road or small aircraft. Arriving at the town's tourist hotel, Crowe thought, "It really is the end of the world." At the reception desk he asked, "What's open at night?" He learned that the general store in town remained open until 6 p.m.[15]

The change of venue had the desired effect. Progress led to the independence of several islands from American trusteeship. In the case of the Northern Marianas, which included Saipan, Rota, and Tinian, the local population elected to seek commonwealth status and remain under the American flag. Throughout the negotiations, Crowe and Williams developed a tight bond and close friendship. Williams worried about Crowe's time away from the Navy and told the four-striper, "I don't want this to ruin your career, and we are going to do something about it." Crowe recalled that Williams wrote a number of "really embellished letters" and called on senior Navy brass to laud Crowe's work. Reflecting decades later in a Naval Historical Foundation oral history, Crowe surmised,

> I don't think Haydn Williams made me an admiral, but he didn't let
> them forget me and he really needled them. He was very generous in
> praise, and he worked hard at it. When he'd write a letter, he'd really
> give it a lot of thought, and he bombarded them. My record was
> replete with endorsements from all kinds of people in the Microne-
> sian business. As I say, that was not probably the most crucial item,
> but it sure was helpful. And he was absolutely ecstatic when I was
> selected for flag rank—and then I had to leave the negotiations.[16]

After serving with Williams for two years, Crowe received orders to return to the Pentagon to become the deputy director of the Strategic Plans, Policy, and Nuclear Systems Division within the office of the Chief of Naval Operations. Meanwhile, Williams forged ahead to complete the negotiations. On February 6, 1975, Secretary of State Henry Kissinger drafted a memorandum for President Gerald Ford on the subject "Micronesia: Final Stage of Negotiations with the Northern Marianas."

In the memorandum, Kissinger discussed a clever method that Williams had proposed, to allow the Department of Defense access to property within Saipan's harbor, should contingencies require it, through the leasing of land that would be used for a memorial park. Though many in Congress preferred outright purchase of the property, Williams had been unable to succeed "principally because of the islanders' almost religious attachment to their land." To develop the memorial park, Williams recommended a one-time $2 million grant to the island. Kissinger supported the request by stating, "The device of a memorial park would make the land more readily available in an emergency and would satisfy local political needs." The president approved the recommendations.[17]

Although the memorial park concept served to preserve basing space in the event of a military contingency, Williams did envision the need for space to commemorate the struggle for Saipan and the Battle of the Philippine Sea that had been fought three decades earlier. Though he returned to continue his leadership at the Asia Foundation, Williams retained an interest in the memorial park and worked with the National Park Service (NPS), which assumed responsibility for its maintenance, and the ABMC, for the placement of markers on the site. On June 15, 1994, marking the fiftieth anniversary of the American landings on Saipan, the Memorial Court of Honor and Flag Circle were dedicated. Surrounding the American flag and the flags of the various services, twenty-six granite panels were inscribed with the names of 5,204 service personnel who lost their lives during the bloody campaign.[18]

A year later on Veterans Day, the ABMC dedicated the Saipan American Memorial and Carillon Bell Tower to commemorate Americans and Chamorros who died during the liberation of Saipan, Tinian, and Guam from June 15 to August 11, 1944. In contrast to the Memorial Court of Honor, this memorial featured a twelve-foot rectangular obelisk of rose granite and an adjoining carillon bell tower.[19]

Admiral Crowe retired as chairman of the Joint Chiefs of Staff in September 1989, having kept in close contact with Ambassador Williams following the Micronesian negotiations. Admiral Crowe's executive assistant, John Bitoff, first met the ambassador when the latter visited Crowe in Naples in 1980, during Crowe's tour in command of NATO forces in Southern Europe. Once

Crowe received orders to command all of the U.S. forces in the Pacific, the bond between Crowe and Williams only tightened. In January 1984, Jack Baldwin, now a rear admiral, hosted Williams on his flagship, the aircraft carrier USS *Kitty Hawk*, en route to the western Pacific via Pearl Harbor, site of Admiral Crowe's headquarters. Leaving the carrier in Hawaii, Williams was in turn hosted by Crowe in his quarters. Their relationship was such that Crowe's daughter, Bambi, was at one point employed by the Asia Foundation. Crowe had followed the ambassador's passionate efforts to memorialize those who had fought at Saipan a half century earlier. Understanding that an effort was in its embryonic stages to honor all of those who served during World War II, and with the change of administrations coming in late 1992, Williams approached Crowe to express an interest in serving with the ABMC. As a retired four-star who had broken ranks with most of his contemporaries to endorse Bill Clinton for the presidency of the United States, Crowe had influence with the new commander in chief.[20]

Crowe's support for Clinton raised eyebrows because the admiral had been appointed to lead the nation's military by President Ronald Reagan. However, he did have some issues with Reagan's successor, George H. W. Bush. For example, Bush chose to sack one of Crowe's regional commanders over Crowe's objection, waiting for the admiral to depart on an overseas trip to allow Secretary of Defense Dick Cheney to deliver the pink slip. The victim, Southern Command's Gen. Frederick F. Woerner, had been quoted in the *New York Times* as being critical toward the administration during a regional Chamber of Commerce Q&A session in Panama. Hardly the case, Crowe determined, once the context of Woerner's statement was heard in a recording.[21]

According to his memoir, what drew Crowe to Clinton was the nation's economic and social problems as well as a "terrible divisiveness isolating so many citizens from the great American community that makes us a people rather than [an] assortment of factions." Following a meeting with the presidential candidate, who had no service background, and a quartet of senior retired leaders (including Crowe) to discuss military issues, Crowe continued his role as an adviser to the candidate. The admiral determined that, contrary to opinions expressed in some quarters, "Clinton was in no sense antimilitary."[22]

Thus, on September 19, 1992, Admiral Crowe formally endorsed William J. Clinton at a rally in Little Rock. Soon thereafter, Crowe reached out to General Woerner, who had settled at Boston University as a faculty member in the Department of International Relations. Still annoyed by his dismissal, the retired four-star had also been bothered by a cadre of retired senior officers who had endorsed President Bush simply on the rationale that Governor Clinton's lack of military service made him unfit to serve as commander in chief. Woerner, noting that other presidents without military backgrounds had served, weighed in to support Clinton's candidacy. Other retired flag and general officers also expressed support for the candidate of the Democratic Party. Among the names listed in an October 12, 1992, press release besides Crowe and Woerner were two retired U.S. Army brigadier generals, Douglas Kinnard and Evelyn "Pat" Foote, and Brig. Gen. Gail Reals, USMC. Both Foote and Reals were path-breaking women in their respective services, with Reals being the first female to be promoted to brigadier general in the history of the Marine Corps.[23]

Elected as the forty-second commander in chief, President Clinton had the prerogative to appoint friends, party faithful, and other deserving candidates to a plethora of cabinet posts, secretarial positions, ambassadorships, judicial vacancies, and other positions in the federal hierarchy. At a gathering in Washington, General Woerner remembered chatting with Samuel Richard "Sandy" Berger, the new deputy national security advisor, about his interest in serving in the Clinton administration. Woerner didn't think he was over-reaching in seeking an ambassadorial appointment to either a Central American or South American country, an area of the globe he had strong familiarity with. Berger left the general hanging, inferring that "they had something bigger in mind."[24]

The new president also had the chore of appointing advisory groups and commissions, including the ABMC, but the latter was low on Clinton's priority list. Well into the second year of his administration, the ABMC still had

holdover appointees from the Reagan and Bush (41) administrations. The
ABMC had initially been founded in 1923 to construct monuments at overseas Army-administered burial grounds, to honor and commemorate those
killed abroad during the U.S. involvement in World War I. Serving as a commissioner on the ABMC was a plum political perk as well as an honor. During
the two world wars, Americans fought, died, and were buried in locations that
today are considered prime tourist destinations. The majority of ABMC's overseas sites, now also including cemeteries, are in European countries such as
France, Italy, Belgium, the Netherlands, and England, as well as Panama and
the Philippines. Though service as a commissioner was uncompensated, the
government did cover travel and berthing costs for the biannual meetings in
Washington and on inspection trips overseas. Of course, the responsibility
associated with the role can be humbling: commissioners are charged with
caretaking of the sacred soil that now serves as the final resting place for those
Americans who paid the ultimate price.[25]

A small staff led by a secretary and an executive director handled the day-
to-day operations of the commission. During the opening months of 1994,
three men hustled to prepare for fiftieth anniversary commemoration events
associated with World War II in Europe. They were the recently appointed
secretary, Lt. Gen. Joseph S. Laposata, USA (Ret.), and the executive director,
Col. Kenneth Pond, USA (Ret.), who had just arrived in Washington after
serving seven years as the ABMC representative at the U.S. Embassy in Rome,
as well as Laposata's memorial project officer, Col. Kevin Kelley of the Army
Corps of Engineers (no relation to the former Marine Corps commandant
and current ABMC chair Gen. P. X. Kelley). Laposata's appointment as the
secretary made sense, considering that when he was on active duty, he had a
reputation as one of the Army's top logisticians.[26] In contrast to Laposata and
Pond, who earned their Army commissions after earning bachelor degrees at
civilian colleges, Kelley was a West Pointer who had been recalled to active
duty from retirement to support the building of the memorial. With an uncle
who had served in the Army Air Forces and a father who had produced

armaments on the home front during the war, Kelley approached his new assignment with a sense of purpose.[27]

Two of ABMC's cemeteries, the Sicily-Rome American Cemetery and the Normandy American Cemetery, would serve as focal points for the commemoration of the fiftieth anniversary of the liberation of Rome on June 4, 1994, and of D-Day at Normandy two days later. In the early months of 1994, the commemorations—as well as the composition of the ABMC, still led by Marine Corps Commandant P. X. Kelley, who had actively campaigned for his opponent—were still not on the radar of President Clinton. However, they loomed as a very big target on the horizon for the American ambassador to France, Pamela Harriman. The title of her biography, published that year, *Life of the Party: The Biography of Pamela Digby Churchill Hayward Harriman*, captured the essence of the widow of the deceased Wall Street tycoon and diplomat W. Averell Harriman. A longtime supporter of the Democratic Party who had opened doors for Governor Clinton during his presidential campaign, Ambassador Harriman saw the forthcoming commemoration as being the most significant event during her tenure in Paris.[28] With ABMC responsible for ten cemeteries and nine monuments in her country, she had no interest in hosting and entertaining a gaggle of Republican appointees led by the former Marine Corps commandant. Frustrated with the inactivity at 1600 Pennsylvania Avenue, Harriman contacted retired foreign service officer Gabriel Guerra-Mondragon, who was known to be on the ABMC candidate list, to see if he could push an article on the matter in the *Washington Post*. When P. X. Kelley opened his copy of that paper on the morning of March 23, he noted the article on page A19 by Al Kamen under the banner "Clinton Could Face Enemy at Omaha Beach." With Kamen's piece explaining that the commission still was the domain of Reagan/Bush-era appointees, Kelley turned to his wife and said, "I'm history."[29]

To replace Kelley, President Clinton had seriously considered former New York governor Hugh L. Carey. Having joined the New York National Guard in 1939, Carey eventually earned a commission as an Army officer and fought in

Europe during the final year of World War II, earning several decorations including a Bronze Star. Leaving active duty as a colonel, Carey earned a law degree and then won a seat in Congress in 1960. Serving two terms as governor of the Empire State from 1975 until 1983, Carey's tenure coincided with the first term of the young governor of Arkansas, Bill Clinton, and the two became acquainted. However, when informed that the post had always been held by a distinguished retired four-star, starting with General of the Armies John J. Pershing, who served as the ABMC chair for a quarter century, the president relented.[30]

Thus, when the White House issued a press release on April 14, 1994, appointing nine members to the commission, Carey's name was included just as a member. Besides Carey, the new commissioners included the three aforementioned brigadier generals, Kinnard, Foote, and Reals. Others noted in the news release included former New York State assemblyman and Navy veteran Rolland E. Kidder; Hawaiian veteran Alfred S. Los Banos; Cook County Democratic Party chairman and former Army Ranger Thomas G. Lyons; sociologist Dr. Brenda L. Moore; and the aforementioned Gabriel Guerra-Mondragon of Maryland.[31]

Ironically, the first time some of the newly appointed commissioners learned of the press release was during the research for this book. Apparently, the media failed to pick up on the White House announcement and the White House personnel office failed to reach out to the selectees. Rolly Kidder remembered getting a call either on May 25 or 26 from the White House director of personnel, Veronica Biggins: "Mr. Kidder, the president would like you to serve on the American Battle Monuments Commission, are you willing to serve?" Kidder shot back, "Does McDonalds have golden arches? Yes!" Biggins then asked if Kidder would have any issues coming down to Washington the following week for the first commission meeting and then flying overseas for the events commemorating the fiftieth anniversary of World War II. Kidder told Biggins he and his wife could make it.

Much to the dismay of Haydn Williams, his name was not listed. His friend Admiral Crowe probed his contacts in the White House. Crowe got back to him and said, "Haydn, the White House called and told me you weren't on the short list and not even on the long list for the ABMC! Are you a Republican?" To which Haydn admitted that he was. "Well, I don't give a damn!" Crowe responded. "I am going to get you on that Commission. You need to be on it."[32]

Crowe's frustration with his apparent inability to land his friend on the commission must have been exacerbated by the knowledge of all of the other strings being pulled on the ambassador's behalf. Perhaps the problem was he was trying too hard!

Crowe had been championing Williams since the end of 1993. With Crowe's backing in early 1994, Williams began drafting letters for a former trustee at the Asia Foundation, Walter H. Shorenstein, to sign, targeting key politicians in Washington. A generous contributor to the Democratic Party, Shorenstein fired off letters to Clinton adviser Bruce Lindsey, Senators Dianne Feinstein, George Mitchell, J. Bennett Johnston, and Sam Nunn, as well as House Speaker Tom Foley. Crowe sent a similar request to Rep. Nancy Pelosi. All obligingly fired off endorsement letters to the White House. Hearing nothing, at the end of February a Williams-authored Shorenstein letter took aim at the top. Responding on March 8, President Clinton thanked Shorenstein and said he passed the letter to his director of presidential personnel, Veronica Biggins. A few days day later Clinton's assistant national security advisor, Sandy Berger, received a missive from Rep. Dick Gephardt. As March turned to April, still nothing! At Williams' behest, Senator Barbara Boxer sent a letter to the president, dated April 11. Three days later came the White House press release sans Williams. On April 28, Biggins wrote to Boxer, copying Williams, to say, "I am pleased to let you know that your insights and support have been carefully noted." Perhaps some headway?[33]

In late May up in Boston, General Woerner received a phone call inviting him to serve as the new chair with one small caveat—he would invite Governor Carey to serve as the vice chairman. Offered an opportunity to continue service to the nation, Woerner accepted. Subsequently on May 27, 1994, the White House issued a press release announcing Woerner's appointment along

with F. Haydn Williams. Notified before the announcement, Williams prepared for the forthcoming trip to Europe.[34]

Most of the reconstituted ABMC gathered on May 30 at a hotel near
Dulles International Airport, in time for Laposata, Pond, and Kelley to provide guidance for the memorable week ahead in Italy and France. Arriving in
Rome, the new commissioners were bussed to Nettuno, to the Sicily-Rome
American Cemetery located near Anzio. There they served as a backdrop for
an impressive ceremony at the ABMC-administered hallowed grounds, which
served as the final resting spot for 7,862 Americans who came to liberate Italy
and made the ultimate sacrifice. More than a thousand of their surviving comrades made the cross-Atlantic trip to observe their president as he paid his
respects to the fallen and to receive his words of thanks. As a cannon salute
cracked through the muggy air, and a military ensemble played Chopin's
Funeral March, a somber President Clinton raised his right arm to salute survivors in attendance. "You cannot leave memory to chance.... [W]e are the
sons and daughters of the world they saved." The occasion had personal meaning for the president, whose father had also fought in Italy then returned to
the States only to tragically lose his life in an automobile accident three
months prior to the birth of his son. Joining the president for the ceremony
were four senators who had also fought in the bloody Italian campaign—
Robert Dole, Daniel Inouye, Ernest Hollings, and Claiborne Pell. Following
the laying of a wreath at the memorial by President Clinton and Italian
president Oscar Luigi Scalfaro, the attendees were impressed by a flyover of
American and Italian combat aircraft.[35]

As the ceremony concluded, the new commissioners took the opportunity
to get acquainted with the seventy-seven-acre property and view the architecture, sculptures, and various inscriptions. Observing his new colleague Haydn
Williams jotting notes into a small journal, Rolly Kidder asked, "Haydn, what
are you taking notes about?" Williams responded, "Some of the architecture and inscriptions here might be helpful to us building the World War II
memorial."

Apparently, Kidder had missed the memo about the 1993 legislation that directed ABMC to find a site, design, raise funds for, and then build a national World War II memorial in Washington. Dumbfounded by this revelation, Kidder pressed Williams for details and learned that the mandate to build a memorial was what had motivated him to seek an appointment to the commission. "If I have enough in me, I want to make this my last 'hurrah,'" stated Williams.[36]

Arriving in France, the commissioners were joined by Brigadier General Foote, who could not make the trip to Italy due to a prior commitment. The commissioners then traveled on to the Normandy American Cemetery to commemorate the fiftieth anniversary of the date marking the beginning of the liberation of France. There they watched as President Clinton provided heartfelt oratory to thousands of Americans and their allies who had returned to the beaches that were once designated Utah, Omaha, Juno, Gold, and Sword. Larger in scale than the Sicily-Rome American Cemetery, the ABMC resting ground on the French coast covers some 172.5 acres and is home to 9,380 graves of fallen Americans. Undoubtedly, in the aftermath of the emotional ceremonies, Williams made notes of the memorial structure, which consists of a semicircular colonnade with loggia on facing sides featuring maps and narratives of the events of June 6, 1944. The focal point of the structure—a bronze statue depicting the *Spirit of American Youth Rising from the Waves*—overlooks a reflecting pool.[37]

With the exception of Haydn Williams, who shared an inkling of what was ahead to Rolly Kidder, the commissioners on the trip had yet to be briefed on the forthcoming assignment. Even Fred Woerner recalled that he was oblivious to the magnitude of the project that had been legislated for ABMC. Following the events at Normandy, all but one of the commissioners flew home to their respective states to enjoy the summer, with a "save the date" notice of September 29. The one commissioner who stayed behind was Williams, having volunteered to inspect the Suresnes American Cemetery and Memorial overlooking Paris before his departure.[38]

Returning to San Francisco, Williams had barely enough time to go through his correspondence before he was again airborne, this time heading west over the Pacific, reaching Saipan after a few connecting flights to attend the June 15 dedication of the Memorial Court of Honor and Flag Circle—a project in which he had played an instrumental role. There he was joined by Colonel Kelley, who had flown ahead to conduct advance work on behalf of the new ABMC commissioner. Upon returning to the States, Williams did not sit back to revel in his recent success. In Boston, General Woerner received a call to see if he would host the meeting of a small contingent consisting of Ambassador Williams, Governor Carey, and a member of the ABMC staff. At the meeting, Williams brought out the congressional legislation assigning ABMC the responsibility of siting, designing, funding, and building the memorial. The legislation called for the creation of a memorial advisory board, following a model that had been used to support the building of the Korean War Veterans Memorial, which was on track to be dedicated during the following summer. President Clinton was soon to announce his presidential appointments to this new body. What would be their responsibilities?[39]

The informal meeting served as a wake-up call for Woerner. However, thanks to the discussions, he now had a grasp of the challenge and a vision for the way ahead. Williams was not done for the summer; he coordinated with Laposata and Kelley to take on another inspection trip to England, Netherlands, Belgium, and Luxembourg to report on the upkeep of the facilities there and to make notes of the architecture.[40]

Finally, the new commissioners reconvened on September 29 with the top agenda item being the building of a World War II memorial in the nation's capital.

The second gathering and first formal meeting of the new commission occurred exactly a month after Williams had celebrated his seventy-fifth birthday with his wife Margaret. Having retired five years earlier from his quarter-century tenure as the president of the Asia Foundation, Williams could have spent his remaining days at his Pacific Heights penthouse perched atop of

2200 Pacific Ave., enjoying breathtaking views of San Francisco and the bay. Instead, for the next six years he would commute forth and back across the country to attend forty-seven Site and Design Committee meetings, some thirty public hearings, and biannual meetings of the ABMC, as well as travel around the world to inspect American military cemeteries in the service of his nation. He would continue to do so after he was replaced in his official capacity, for many years into the twenty-first century and well into his nineties. Essentially taking on a full-time job, Williams refused to adapt to the latest technology, spurning computers and e-mail. Instead, the senior statesman carried with him yellow legal pads and an assortment of number 2 pencils to copy down thoughts, write memorandums for the record, summarize meetings, outline strategies, and craft correspondence.

Given the amount of time he spent in the air between Washington and San Francisco, Williams had ample time to compose, and upon touchdown he would transmit his writings via facsimile. In the case of correspondence, the staff at the ABMC was on constant standby to type his penciled prose onto official stationery for his signature. For Laposata, Pond, Kelley, and their successors, Williams would be "high maintenance." Whereas in 1994, personal computers were still somewhat of a novelty, in 2004 colleague Pat Foote wrote an e-mail to her design committee compadres asking, "Perhaps it's time we chip in to buy Haydn a computer so he can join the 21st century."[41]

Still, Kidder remembered Williams at that first meeting as a transformative figure. "He was skillful, diplomatic and had a magnetic personality—he was not a person you could say 'No' to." By that second meeting, Williams had lobbied Woerner on the need for a small subcommittee to tackle the siting and the design of the memorial, suggesting that he and Governor Carey were ideally suited for it. Woerner agreed. On October 24, Woerner sent Williams a letter inviting him to join with Pat Foote on a committee of commissioners to be led by Governor Carey. Failing to reach the general by phone, Williams faxed Woerner a response, stating, "It would be an honor."[42]

In contrast, Foote was stunned when she received her letter stating she would be paired with Williams to work for Carey. Foote had grown up during the Depression in North Carolina. Her parents moved to the nation's capital during World War II to work for the federal government. After graduating high school, Foote performed clerical work at the FBI to raise money for college and took the advice of an uncle to attend Wake Forest University, receiving a BA in sociology in 1953. Foote returned to work for the FBI, then for the *Washington Daily News*, and then for Group Hospitalization, only to find that the glass ceiling those days was only a few inches off the floor:

> There was little upper mobility for women in those years. Women would not [be] permitted to be FBI agents; the *Washington Daily News* would only assign me to the staff to write about food and fashion; and at Group Hospitalization, I could not be a salesperson or sales manager. After all, I was a woman.[43]

Frustrated, Foote began to look at the military service for a career option and settled on the Army. Commissioned as a first lieutenant in December 1959, Foote made the most of the opportunities provided, given the congressional prohibition against assigning women to combat roles—a prohibition she would work to overturn. Her performance, as she rose through the ranks, broke down barriers. She served as the first female public relations officer in Vietnam, the first female faculty member appointed to the U.S. Army War College, the first female brigade commander in Europe, the first female deputy inspector general for the Department of the Army, and the first female commander of Fort Belvoir, Virginia. When promoted to brigadier general in 1986, Foote was only the fourth female to reach that rank.

In retrospect, Foote's appointment to the ABMC should not have come as too much of a surprise. Before joining the faculty at the Army War College, she had been a student there, and her faculty adviser was the director of the Latin American Studies department—Col. Fred Woerner. The former student had continued to impress Woerner as both advanced in the Army. Woerner's selection of Foote would prove to be an astute move.[44]

Chapter Two

LOCATION! LOCATION! LOCATION!

1994–95

C OINCIDING WITH the September 29 gathering of the new commissioners was the announcement from the White House of the World
War II Memorial Advisory Board (MAB). The dozen individuals
named represented a true cross-section of Americans having a connection with
World War II who also had capabilities to contribute to the task at hand. On
paper it was a formidable group.

The individual selected to chair the board, Peter Wheeler, had served as
Georgia's commissioner of veterans' affairs for more than four decades. An
Army veteran of World War II, he retained his uniform to serve with the Geor-
gia National Guard, retiring in 1978 as a brigadier general. Perhaps having held
the same position since 1952 had made him a bit complacent, for General
Woerner would be underwhelmed by his leadership.

Rear Adm. Ming E. Chang provided some naval perspective to the board.
Decorated for combat in Vietnam, Chang capped his thirty-four-year career as
the Navy's inspector general. He would eventually join with Haydn Williams
on several of the design meetings of the memorial.

Another individual who would sit in on future design meetings, Miguel Encinias, flew seventy missions with the Army Air Force during World War II before being shot down and held in Germany as a POW for fifteen months. After his homecoming, he remained in the newly created U.S. Air Force to serve during the Korean and Vietnam conflicts.

Along with Encinias, William C. Ferguson Sr. also took pride in his Army Air Force wings of silver as a former Tuskegee Airman. As the publisher and author of *Black Flyers of World War II*, Ferguson symbolized how the war would help drive social change.

Yet another aviator, Jon A. Mangis, served as one of Peter Wheeler's counterparts as Oregon's director and CEO of the Department of Veterans' Affairs. Unlike Encinias and Ferguson, Mangis did not see time in the sky during World War II, having served during Vietnam. However, Mangis had long maintained a personal connection with the ABMC because his father, a B-17 pilot shot down and killed in combat, rested in peace at the ABMC cemetery at Margraaten in the Netherlands. Mangis would contribute an idea for an important design element of the final memorial.

In contrast, Jess Hay had served as CEO of a Texas-based financial corporation for nearly three decades. Associated with numerous cultural and educational institutions and serving on several corporate and political boards, Hay could be expected to assist in the fundraising realm. General Woerner would be effusive in praise for Hay's contributions to what proved to be a phenomenal fundraising effort.

The name that many World War II Army veterans would recognize, Bill Mauldin, had served in the infantry before gaining fame as a correspondent for *Stars and Stripes*. The creator of the cartoon *Willy and Joe*, which offered a G.I. perspective of the war, continued working as a political cartoonist after the war and covered the Korean, Vietnamese, and Arab-Israeli conflicts as a civilian correspondent. With his best days behind him, Mauldin would lend his presence at fundraising efforts and make appearances to testify on Capitol Hill.

Joining Mauldin as another veteran "ground pounder," Robert Moorhead had also served in Europe with the Army during World War II and then had joined the Indiana Army National Guard, rising to the rank of major general.

While Mauldin and Moorhead had served in Europe, John W. "Bill" Murphy fought with the Marines in the Pacific. Wounded, Murphy had advocated for veterans for nearly a half century and was then serving as the national vice commander of the American Legion. Murphy would prove to be an ideal liaison to the numerous veterans' organizations, whose members numbered in the millions.

Along with the nine males, President Clinton appointed three women.

The youngest selectee, at the age of twenty-six, was Melissa A. Durbin. Committed to seeing her aging grandfather Roger Durbin's dream become reality, the young lady had just attained a master of arts degree from Bowling Green State University and was an art history teacher.[1]

Perhaps the appointment raising the most eyebrows was that of Sarah McClendon. With a journalism degree from the University of Missouri, McClendon had served in the Women's Army Corps during World War II as a public affairs officer before joining the Washington office of the *Philadelphia Daily News* in 1944. In a male-dominated profession, McClendon struck out on her own by creating the McClendon News Service, which offered coverage in the nation's capital for smaller market newspapers that could not afford a D.C. bureau. As a member of the White House Press Corps, she had covered every president from Franklin D. Roosevelt to Bill Clinton, often drawing their disdain. Hardly the wallflower, McClendon shouted questions in a way that caused her colleagues to cringe. President George H. W. Bush once warned her that "the loudest voice doesn't get recognized as it isn't fair to the others." She was direct and hard-hitting. Fellow correspondent Helen Thomas remembered, "She made the veins stand out in Eisenhower's head, because he would get so mad." McClendon once confessed that the Secret Service warned her against pointing her pen at President Richard Nixon when making queries. President Clinton would later remark, after McClendon's passing, "I hope

St. Peter is prepared for the kinds of questions that nearly a dozen presidents had to face."[2]

No doubt her appointment was made in grudging respect and in recognition that the campaign to build the memorial would need support in the media. However, the eighty-four-year-old sage would not be content to serve as a mouthpiece for the ABMC World War II Memorial effort. She was determined to play a role in its siting, and this would conflict with the vision of one of the ABMC commissioners—Haydn Williams.

In the White House press release, the shortest statement mentioned a woman from Sarasota:

> Helen Fagin of Florida is an Eastern European Jewish Holocaust survivor who arrived in the United States in 1946. Recently retired as a Professor of English Literature, she has chaired the Education Committee of the Holocaust Museum in Washington. She has taught courses in Literature of the Holocaust, Roots of Anti-Semitism and the Holocaust and Its Aftermath.

Now eighty-two, the elderly Jewish immigrant, who hailed from Radomsko, Poland, had experienced peril comparable to that of her male World War II counterparts, who had fought the Germans and Japanese on the ground, in the skies, and at sea. The middle daughter of Soloman and Ewa Neimark, Helen experienced some anti-Semitism in the predominantly Catholic nation. With limited public schooling options available thanks to her religion, Helen and her older and younger sisters attended a private Jewish gymnasium for most of their youth. She had been admitted to the restricted Jagiellonian University in Kraków when the Germans attacked. She recalled that the day after the German invasion of Poland on September 1, 1939, her home was bombed and destroyed by the Luftwaffe.

Helen's enclave was turned into a ghetto. In October 1942, Helen and two sisters hid while the Nazis arrested her parents and transported them to a concentration camp. Shortly thereafter, Helen's two sisters managed to escape Radomsko. When the Nazis decided to eliminate the Jewish ghetto in January 1943, the teenage Helen broke for it during a march to the railroad station. She was reunited with her sisters, and all three young women benefited from an active Polish underground, which provided Helen and her older sister with false identities and employment and placed the youngest sister with a Catholic orphanage. Her parents and others of her immediate family all perished in the Holocaust. With the Russian army clearing Poland of the ever-looming Nazi threat, the Neimark sisters eventually made their way to Bad Gastein, a displaced persons camp run by the American/United Nations Refugee Agency in Austria. Helen had visions of migrating to Palestine to join up with distant relatives. However, a U.S. Army lieutenant was smitten with Helen's elder sister, and that marriage provided a ticket for all three sisters to emigrate to the New World, arriving in New York on the troopship *American Flasher*. Helen recalled that she arrived "without any identity papers, luggage, nor understanding of the English language, but with one ambition—that of surviving as a human being, with dignity."

Settling in Brooklyn, Helen became a seamstress in the alterations department of a ladies' apparel store, while studying English with the help of a German-English dictionary and the *New York Times*. Helen met her future husband, Sidney, at a New York City dance in May 1947. While dating the former Army Air Force cryptographer, who had left the service to join his father's construction company, she took night courses to attain a high school equivalency certificate and then attended a graduate evening course at Brooklyn College on the "Derivation of the English Language." In late 1948 they were wed. The birth of her daughter Judith in 1950 coincided with the arrival of her citizenship papers. Fagin delightfully recalled, "What joy! I became an American citizen and gave birth to an American citizen, as well!" During the following year, the Fagins moved to Miami to join other family members, and Sidney found success as a contractor.[3] Following the birth of her son Gary, the mother of two continued her education at Miami-Dade Junior College, graduating with honors. She then received a scholarship to the University of Miami, where she was persuaded to pursue a major in literature.

After receiving her MA, the Jewish immigrant who had arrived on America's shores a few years earlier nonconversant in the lingua franca, was offered a position of freshman English instructor at the University of Miami.

A pivotal point in Fagin's professional/personal life was meeting Elie Wiesel, who insisted that she consider teaching classes about the Holocaust. She remembered him telling her, "If you and I as survivors will not do it, we will leave it to the IMAGINATION of others to tell the story."

From then on Fagin became identified with Holocaust studies, and soon was asked to develop a curriculum in Jewish studies at the University of Miami, where she became the program director.

Then Wiesel called her in the late 1970s asking for help "with creating a future important institution of remembrance of the Holocaust." Thus, she would chair the Holocaust Education Committee for what would eventually become the National Holocaust Memorial Museum, and later served with that museum's content and academic committees.[4]

Besides chairing the Education Committee at the National Holocaust Museum in Washington, one piece of information missing from the White House announcement was Fagin's lead role in the siting and design of the substantial Holocaust Memorial located at Miami Beach. She recalled, "I was considering taking early retirement from the University of Miami, when a group of friends approached me with an idea of building a memorial for victims of the Holocaust . . . in Miami Beach." Having longed for years to memorialize her lost parents, Fagin jumped to it. As vice president and director of the Holocaust Memorial Committee, she oversaw the selection process that brought in Miami native Kenneth Treister to design and fabricate a sober installation located in the heart of one of the nation's top recreational destinations. Dedicated on February 4, 1990, the $3 million memorial centered on a bronze arm stretching toward the heavens, fingers opened, with its wrist scarred with a concentration camp number. The 42-foot limb, rising from a serene reflecting pool, appeared engulfed in flames as life-size naked, emaciated humanoid figures clung on to the base of the structure, attempting to emerge from the abyss.

The stirring memorial would have its critics. "It is a grotesque aberration, a pock on the landscape, a polluter of public space that offends any sense of dignity," observed Paula Harper, an art historian and one of Fagin's fellow professors at the University of Miami. The *Miami Herald*'s art critic, Helen Kohen, also rendered a harsh rebuke: "The memorial is ugly. There's nothing welcoming about it. I know people will say neither were the ovens, but we're not talking about ovens. We're talking about art."

Fagin offered no apologies: "It is the hand of a mother asking for mercy for her child, of the doomed reaching for help from the darkness of a cattle car, of the hungry begging for bread, of the old searching for God and asking, 'Why?'"[5]

With her experience in shepherding the creation of a substantial memorial and her fortitude to stand up to criticism, Fagin would endear herself to Williams on the forthcoming World War II Memorial. Reflecting decades later, General Woerner would rank Fagin along with Jess Hay as the two MAB members who contributed the most to making the World War II Memorial a reality.

Toward the end of the month Fagin and her colleagues received correspondence from Colonel Kelley inviting them to the first gathering of the new presidential advisory board. On December 1, 1994, the group met at the National Guard Memorial Building near the ABMC offices in the Pulaski Building,[6] just a short distance from Union Station in the nation's capital. After an hour of socializing over a catered luncheon spread, the group took their assigned seats in a large meeting room. At the head table, Governor Carey and Chairman Wheeler took the two center chairs. To the right of Carey sat ABMC commissioners Williams and Foote. Colonel Kelley and Lieutenant General Laposata occupied the seats to Wheeler's left. Following Wheeler's welcoming and introductions, Laposata provided an orientation about the ABMC and then Kelley briefed the gathering about the World War II Memorial project. Kelley also recommended to Chairman Wheeler that his group form a subcommittee to parallel the ABMC subcommittee that had been created for the project. Wheeler acted on this suggestion. Representing the World War II Memorial subcommittee to which Woerner had delegated the charge of making the memorial a reality, Carey, Williams, and Foote looked on during the Wheeler-led discussions, concerned that this new body was not getting good guidance on its responsibilities, despite the signing of a memorandum of understanding between the MAB and the ABMC that delineated the aspects of the relationship. Williams also likely pondered the appointment of McClendon to head up a MAB site selection subcommittee.[7]

Williams stayed behind the next day and met with Laposata and Kelley to express his concerns, and then called General Woerner on December 5 to warn him of the problems that lay ahead unless coordination between the MAB and ABMC was tightened.

Addressing the ambassador's concerns, on December 8, Kelley issued a memo asking to schedule a joint meeting in the new year to look over potential sites that were being generated by the National Park Service (NPS), which had jurisdiction over the public lands in the core Mall area. As Kelley worked with the representatives from the two bodies to set a date in January, he also facilitated a meeting on December 13 to discuss promotion and budget. With MAB members Chang and Moorhead in attendance, it was understood that the commemorative coin legislation was hardly going to generate the needed income for what was seen as a $50 million project. Proposals to have the federal government underwrite this cost would prove to be wishful thinking.[8]

As if Kelley wasn't being kept busy enough over the holiday season, he was also exchanging faxes with Williams on an evolving concept statement outlining the purposes of the memorial. The statement concluded: "These purposes dictate that the World War II Memorial be prominent and accessible in location, inspirational in content, inclusive in representation, and symbolic of the American people's past and continued patriotism and dedication to liberty, equality, and democracy."

Also germane to the task at hand, Kelley had been in touch with Lt. Gen. Claude M. Kicklighter, USA (Ret.), the executive director of the U.S. 50th Anniversary of World War II Commemoration Committee, to discuss the concept of having the president dedicate a World War II Memorial site on or about Veterans Day in 1995 as the culminating event of the ongoing commemoration.

This objective added additional urgency to the quest of identifying a site. As the landlord over most of the green expanses stretching from the Capitol Building to the Lincoln Memorial, the NPS had followed the congressional legislation authorizing the memorial to be constructed on its property and decided to be proactive in offering locations that would avoid controversy.

The face of the NPS would be John G. Parsons, the associate director for the National Capital Region. In addition, Parsons served as the chair for the National Capital Memorial Commission (NCMC)—an agency established under the Commemorative Works Act of 1986 with the statutory authority to reject or approve the siting of memorials and monuments—one of three commissions having approval authority over the final site and design. Over time, Williams would size Parsons up as a skillful Washington bureaucrat with chameleon qualities, being adept at surveying the dominant political winds and adjusting course as necessary. The two men initially met at the first joint meeting of the ABMC and MAB subcommittees held on January 20, 1995. Besides Williams, Foote, and Carey, Commissioner Rolland Kidder joined the ABMC contingent for what proved to be a cold, misty day in the nation's capital.

Governor Carey chaired the morning session at the ABMC Pulaski Building headquarters and offered welcoming remarks. Following a map orientation by Colonel Kelley, the group received a pitch from Parsons previewing the hoops they would need to jump through to meet the approval of the NCMC. Williams took note of some of the sage advice being given: "The process needs cooperation from Day One. . . . Think about a program and get a handle on what is wanted." Likewise, the group heard from the secretary of the

Commission of Fine Arts (CFA), Charles H. Atherton, about how planning in the nation's capital had evolved since 1790. Before heading out, the group was asked to consider locations that: (1) already featured plazas, fountains, and pools that could be repurposed into a memorial; (2) determine if they wanted a contemplative secluded site or a location "on a visually important axial location in the city plan"; and finally, (3) avoid encroaching on an existing memorial. The group then boarded vans and proceeded to the sites that had been picked out by the NPS.

The group visited the following designated sites:

1. An area on the Mall immediately west of the Capitol Reflecting Pool.
2. A location on the northeast shore of the Tidal Basin juxtaposed with the sight line between the White House and the Jefferson Memorial.
3. West Potomac Park, southeast of the Lincoln Memorial and overlooking the Potomac.
4. Constitution Gardens—the former site of the Main Navy building on the west side of 17th Street, south of Constitution Avenue.
5. A site northeast of the Washington Monument and close to the National Museum of American History, a location that eventually would host the National Museum of African American History and Culture.
6. Freedom Plaza, located on Pennsylvania Avenue between 13th and 14th streets NW.

The tour group was also shown a seventh location across the river in Arlington—the Marine Corps Headquarters at Henderson Hall, along the southern edge of Arlington Cemetery. However, though the Marines had hinted at a potential move, it was not to occur in the near future and the site was pulled from the list. As of 2019, the Marines still occupy Henderson Hall, though the Navy Annex buildings across the way have been demolished. Now the site is marked with the majestic array of three stainless steel arcs memorializing the service and sacrifices of those who served in the Air Force.[9]

Sarah McClendon banged out her report to the MAB on her manual typewriter, listing the numerous restrictions that limited potential site choices, such as underground tunnels, prohibited use of the grounds of the Washington Memorial, and taboos against blocking sight lines within certain corridors. She also informed her colleagues that Atherton had strongly hinted that the CFA endorsed the Freedom Plaza location. As for McClendon, she was intrigued by the Capitol Reflecting Pool site.[10]

In contrast, Haydn Williams was underwhelmed with all the locations shown. However, Kidder sensed the ambassador had a "Eureka!" moment when the group walked across the Mall from the Constitution Gardens location, to look at the gazebo-shaped structure that memorialized the D.C. Veterans of World War I. Returning to the Constitution Gardens site, the group walked past the deteriorated Olmsted Rainbow Pool, whose fountains were long out of service. Kidder observed Williams pausing. Looking at the sweeping vista, with the Lincoln Memorial to the west and the Washington Monument towering to the east, Kidder recalled Williams saying, "Here is where the World War II Memorial should be. Here on the axis of the National Mall between Lincoln and Washington, we are memorializing the most significant event for the country in the twentieth century; this would be the most appropriate place for the memorial."[11]

Following lunch at the Fort Myers Officers Club, the group made their way back to the Pulaski Building for an afternoon session chaired by Williams, with the objective of creating a short list. The group made little headway except to reach agreement that an outside expert should be brought in for consultation.

Returning to Sarasota, Helen Fagin typed up a memo for her colleagues, asking, "I respectfully request we become a client," and sought recommendations for a site selection consultant. In doing so she promoted her candidate, an Alexandria-based firm that had worked on the Vietnam Memorial. Fagin also urged the group to hire Jay Brodie at RTKL to assist with agency approvals and Stanton Eckstut of the New York–based Ehrenkrantz & Eckstut to provide architectural help. "From my previous experience with the U.S. Holocaust Memorial Museum, I strongly believe this deliberative process will prevent us from falling victim to costly changes later." On the same day, she posted a letter to Colonel Kelley recommending that selection of an outside consultant be added to the forthcoming meeting agenda being prepared for March 2.[12]

Unbeknownst to Fagin, Kelley had already taken the initiative to contract with the Washington firm of architect Davis A. Buckley to consult about site selection. Having arrived in Washington two decades earlier from Yale with a contract to assess the facility needs of the House of Representatives, Buckley permanently planted his flag in the nation's capital by founding the firm bearing his name in 1979. A decade and a half later, his firm had accrued an impressive portfolio of projects dealing with historic preservation, memorials, educational facilities, and land-use planning. Germane to the task at hand, Buckley's firm completed the National Law Enforcement Officers Memorial in 1991 on E Street and had been selected to build the Japanese American Memorial to Patriotism During World War II, which would be sited at Louisiana Avenue and D Street. In mid-February, Williams contacted Buckley to discuss his thoughts about the Rainbow Pool, suggesting the possibility that the Constitution Gardens site could be pushed south to incorporate the Olmsted landmark. Williams later recorded: "What I had in mind was the pool being the memorial's centerpiece. The central east-west vortex would be kept open and the memorial's architectural elements would be on the north and south ends of the pool." Buckley subsequently broached the issue with Parsons and reported back a negative reaction.[13]

To Helen Fagin's delight, when the joint group reconvened on March 2 at the Pulaski Building, Davis Buckley was on hand to provide a pros-and-cons evaluation of the six NPS proposed sites. Following the opening remarks by Governor Carey and Colonel Kelley, the guest presenter offered his observations. Regarding Site #1 on the Mall west of the Capitol Reflecting Pool, Buckley liked the location on the Mall and the relationship with the Grant Memorial to the east and other buildings along the Mall's corridors.

He cautioned that, since an interstate highway lay immediately below, digging was restricted, and any proposed design would have to be symmetrical. Buckley was more negative on Site #2 on the Tidal Basin, noting that it would conflict with the paddleboat concession and was a bit out of the way. He had a similar assessment for Site #3, West Potomac Park along the Potomac. Buckley observed that, although the relationship with the nearby FDR Memorial would provide historical linkage, the site would experience an engineering challenge similar to that of Site #1, because the FDR Memorial rested on some nine hundred pilings that were pounded down 80 to 100 feet deep. Coming to Site #4, the Constitution Gardens site, Buckley cited the linkage to the Lincoln and Washington Memorials, the Vietnam Memorial to the immediate west, good public access, the mature landscape, and being central to the monumental core. Rapidly jotting down Buckley's observations on his yellow legal pad, Williams underlined that last point. On the Site #4 diagram handout, Williams doodled structures on the north and south ends of the adjacent Rainbow Pool. For cons, Buckley observed that the site stood on a flood plain, and that traffic noise on 17th Street would affect atmospherics. Site #5, located on the northeast quadrant of the Washington Memorial grounds, was seen as infringing on the 555-foot marble obelisk honoring the first president. Finally, the ABMC consultant turned to the CFA-favored #6 Freedom Plaza site, noting that a vision of two large pillars had been suggested by one of the CFA commissioners he spoke with. On the pro side, Buckley lauded the proximity to the White House and the vista down Pennsylvania Avenue toward the Capitol. However, the site's location away from the monumental core, nearby commercial establishments, and traffic noise were duly noted on the Williams legal pad.[14]

In addition to Buckley's presentation, the group was provided recent annual visitation numbers for 1993 for the various memorials in the district. Whereas several of the Mall memorials hosted upwards of nearly 4 million individuals, it was noted that the National Law Enforcement Memorial, located a mere five blocks north of the Mall, drew only 14,000 visitors.

Following the Buckley presentation, the joint group recessed for lunch and then again convened to determine a preferred site. That night, Sarah McClendon typed out on her manual typewriter her report of the meeting for Chairman Wheeler, which would be shared at the next day's MAB meeting. "I have the honor to report to you today that the Site Selection Committee of the WWII advisory group working under the ABMC voted on these choices for the site of the memorial: First choice Site No. 4; Second choice Site No. 1; Third choice Site No. 5, and alternative Site No. 6." Noting that the Constitution Gardens site had been a unanimous choice, she continued to type out her personal vision for the future structure: "I hope it will be practical, specific in wording and wasting not an inch on anything abstract, too general, or needing interpretation. We have enough bureaucratic language in this city and we do not need now Pentagonese that would surely be non-understandable by people."[15]

The first sentence likely drew the ire of Helen Fagin. When the architect and sculptor of her Miami Beach Holocaust Memorial was asked about his giant arm design, Kenneth Treister responded, "It's up to each person to decide what it means . . . all I wanted to do was to give each person the opportunity to think about it, to give people the chance to understand something that cannot be understood. It's really an impossible challenge."[16]

On March 2, the two women again met as the MAB convened for its second meeting. Under the chairmanship of Peter Wheeler, the focus of the meeting had been to discuss the site selection process and the funding. General Moorhead reported that the December 13 meeting had set a fundraising goal of $50 million. A fundraising study reported that $25 million was all that could be expected from public sources. It was anticipated that Congress would offer matching funds. Williams balked. Earlier, Williams had shared a cab ride with Davis Buckley and Hugh Carey and recalled the former governor asking Buckley how much it would take to build the Lincoln Memorial in 1995 dollars. The ABMC consultant pondered, did some research, and reported back, "$100 million." Williams moved that the revised goal be $100 million.

There were gasps from ABMC staff and others who couldn't conceive of raising that amount of money. Endorsements from Jess Hay and Helen Fagin swayed the group to the new target.

Calling Governor Carey, who had missed the two days of meetings, Williams told him of the new funding goal of $100 million that would be split between private and public sources and of the need to call General Woerner to get full ABMC support for the Site #4 selection. In a follow-on phone call with Colonel Kelley, Williams learned that Kelley and Buckley called on Parsons to discuss the site selections, where they learned that Parsons had favored Site #1 and would object to an educational/interior theater structure on Site #4. When the two emissaries again broached to Parsons the idea of structures flanking the Rainbow Pool, they received a negative response—though he did like the concept for Site #1. Kelley also informed the ambassador that his advocacy for doubling the funding goal had apparently annoyed General Moorhead, who now assumed Williams was also leading the fundraising effort.[17]

On April 2, while he was in San Francisco, Davis Buckley called on Williams at 2200 Pacific Avenue to again review the different sites, with an aim of forging a game plan for a forthcoming hearing scheduled for May 9 before the National Capital Memorial Commission. Buckley received the go-ahead to write the proposal for the NCMC to ask for Site #4. The consultant reminded Williams that Parsons, who had offered up the six sites and who was predisposed to the Capitol Mall site, was chairing the NCMC. Buckley suggested the time had come to bring in a professional public relations firm to help plan strategy and build public support. The next day the phone rang in Kelley's office. The colonel jotted down notes as Williams summed up the meeting he had had with Buckley and requested that Kelley call Governor Carey and General Foote to invite them to the May 9 NCMC meeting. Williams then learned that Carey would be in Europe for festivities marking the fiftieth anniversary of VE Day, thus relegating the NCMC presentation to him.

As Williams prepared for his presentation, Buckley had returned to Washington and again scheduled an appointment to call on Parsons in an effort to nudge him to be open on the Rainbow Pool, offering a carrot in the form of funding to rehabilitate the pool's long-dormant fountains. Parsons welcomed the offer and gave Buckley a heads-up that he should anticipate pressure to select the Freedom Plaza site at the forthcoming hearing.

As the calendar turned to May, Williams and Buckley continued to tweak their presentation scheduled for May 9. Based on his acquaintance with Parsons, Buckley expressed confidence that the NCMC hearing would go well. Buckley's concern was with the Commission of Fine Arts, which, incidentally, hosted the NCMC hearing. Sure enough, following testimony by Williams and Foote before the Parsons-led panel, CFA Secretary Charles Atherton stood before the commission to argue the merits of the Freedom Plaza site. Thanking him for his input, Parsons adjourned the public hearing portion of the session to allow for deliberation.

The decision was not quite what ABMC representatives had hoped for, except that the panel removed the Freedom Plaza site from contention. The ABMC World War II Memorial Committee was asked to take a second look at both the #1 and #4 sites and report back for the next scheduled hearing in June. Disappointed at the outcome in his home court, Atherton warned the ABMC representatives, "It just may be that these two sites you mentioned would not meet the approval of the Commission [of Fine Arts]."[18]

The ruling left Williams a bit perplexed, and he may have contributed to the indecision. Though the memorial committee had voted unanimously on Site #4, he had difficulty in defending the pick when, unlike Site #1, the site lay off to the side of the Mall axis. In reality, Williams had difficulty being enthusiastic about the Constitution Gardens location when his heart was wed to the Rainbow Pool.

Williams remained in Washington because three days later, on May 12, Woerner convened the full ABMC for one of its biannual meetings. There, Williams recounted for his fellow commissioners the progress on site selection and the split decision made by the NCMC. Boarding a bus, the commissioners were driven to the two sites that remained in play. They subsequently voted to affirm approval of the Constitution Gardens site, with the Capitol Reflecting Pool site as the alternative.

For the ambassador, he had just enough time to return to San Francisco to repack his bags before being again airborne, this time with Margaret at his side, on an Air France flight to Paris. In keeping with his commissioner duties, Williams landed in Paris on May 16 and rested a day to adjust for jet lag before being hosted for dinner by Ambassador Harriman. Traveling between Paris and Brussels over the next week, the couple not only inspected ABMC properties in the two countries, but also toured some French military cemeteries, battlefields, and military museums to observe how the tragedy of war and sacrifice was presented. Highlighting the trip on May 21, Williams gave the keynote address during an acceptance ceremony for a carillon that had been installed at the Meuse-Argonne Military Cemetery—the final resting place for 14,246 American soldiers from World War I. Departing Paris mid-day on the 24th, Haydn and Margaret touched down in New York as the day began on the East Coast, thanks to Concorde. After a day in New York, the couple returned to San Francisco.[19]

Once again, reams of paper recommenced coming out of Williams', Buckley's, and Kelley's facsimile machines as the three looked ahead to again going before Parsons' panel in three weeks. Buckley, noting the limitations of building at Site #1, suggested a nearby site near the intersections of Constitution and Pennsylvania Avenues to serve as a counterbalance to the glass-enclosed National Botanical Garden across the way. Williams demurred.

Studying Buckley's latest site summary, Williams underlined the consultant's observation that, "Of utmost concern seems to be the timing of the approval process as it effects the November dedication of the site." Buckley's analysis zeroed in on the Rainbow Pool. Again the ambassador penciled a line under the following passage: "The dominant symmetry of the axis connecting these two monuments [Washington and Lincoln] and the tree-framed vista virtually prescribes that any elements placed between these monuments would need to be symmetrical about the axis." Buckley then proposed framing the

Rainbow Pool with two loggia, which would not interfere with the vista but serve as a forecourt to announce the memorial, comparable in size to the Lincoln and Jefferson memorials, situated on a mound on the Constitution Gardens plot. To further their case for the grounds north of the Rainbow Pool, Buckley reminded Williams that the property had hosted Main Navy for a half century, implying a historical military connection.[20]

Through the first weeks of June, Williams worked and reworked the case statement for the Constitution Gardens site, consulting with Buckley by phone over strategy. Would it make sense to argue for an extension of Site #4 to include the Rainbow Pool before the NCMC, or would it be better to simply get that panel's blessing for the present footprint then seek expansion down the road before the Commission of Fine Arts and the National Capital Planning Commission (NCPC)? Williams worried that a premature extension request could antagonize the park service, which still needed to be sold on the concept.[21]

On June 20 at 1 p.m., John Parsons reconvened the NCMC. This time, Governor Carey was on hand to kick off the ABMC presentation, citing the importance of determining a site, since the president wanted to do a ground dedication ceremony in November. Ambassador Williams, after presenting his concept statement discussing the purpose of the memorial, yielded the floor to General Foote, who discussed the importance of linkage to the Korean War and Vietnam Memorials. Davis Buckley then placed Site #1 and Site #4 in context with the McMillan Union Square Plan of 1901 and subsequent planning documents. Looking at the pros and cons of the two sites, Buckley favored the Constitution Gardens site due to historical context and linkage to the two more recent war memorials. In follow-on questioning, Williams asserted more confidence defending ABMC's preferred choice. Asked about the Rainbow Pool, Williams surmised that a Constitution Gardens choice could allow for a potential "major exploration of the Rainbow Pool." Parsons reminded the petitioners that the Rainbow Pool was off-limits as far as the NPS was concerned. The CFA secretary again weighed in, expressing displeasure with both sites.

"If I had my preference, I would stick this memorial out in the Rainbow Pool and forget Site #4," observed Charles Atherton. Williams took note.[22]

The MAB site advice committee vice chair Sarah McClendon also took notes and drafted a summary report to cohort Helen Fagin detailing the outcome of the NCMC deliberations. This was to again recommend both sites #1 and #4 for consideration at the next CFA and NCPC hearings, which coincided a month later on July 27. McClendon mentioned that she had contacted the chair of the CFA, J. Carter Brown, who argued that the Freedom Plaza site was the best solution. Brown noted that vacant space in the D.C. government building facing the memorial could serve as educational and exhibition spaces.[23]

For Williams, he saw a potential silver lining in the indecision and in Atherton's suggestion to sway Parsons toward the Rainbow Pool site. The ambassador directed Buckley to prepare drawings showing the memorial centered on the Olmsted-designed landmark "with the main vista left unimpeded and with two semicircular architectural elements enclosing the pool on the north and south." Not quite clear on the thinking behind the NCMC's decision, Williams fired off a letter to Parsons on June 29, asking for clarifications on the boundaries of the two sites and inquired if the NPS might be amenable to expanding the boundaries of Site #4 southward.

As the calendar flipped to July, the site conundrum began to attract media attention. Williams was chided in a July 1 piece in the *Washington Post* by architectural critic Ben Forgey, which took aim at his conceptual goal to have the memorial tell the story of World War II: "Memorials are not schools!" Faxes continued to fly forth and back across the country in preparation for the July 27 presentations. Williams had hoped to bring the two commissions together so that the ABMC team could conduct just one briefing. Wishful thinking. Colonel Kelley sent a memo to Williams on July 10 outlining the schedule for the 27th, which kicked off with an early-morning joint site visit by both commissions. There would be two separate hearings, with a 10 a.m. session with the CFA and after lunch an afternoon session with the NCPC.[24]

On July 14, Parsons called Williams to discuss the letter sent from San Francisco two weeks earlier. The ambassador recorded a somewhat productive give-and-take, as he affirmed that Parsons agreed with his opposition of the Freedom Plaza site—certainly to be discussed at the CFA hearing, and that Parsons and the park service staff were leaning in favor of the Constitution Gardens site. As for expanding the Constitution Gardens footprint, Parsons remained noncommittal on the phone, knowing that a letter would be sent four days later to ABMC stating the Rainbow Pool remained not in play.[25]

For Lieutenant General Laposata and the staff of the ABMC, the date the CFA/NCPC selected to host their hearings—Thursday, July 27—happened to coincide with the forty-second anniversary of the cessation of hostilities on the Korean peninsula and, more significantly, the official afternoon dedication of the Korean War Memorial, which would be spearheaded by President Bill Clinton and President Kim Young Sam of South Korea. Add in a World War II Memorial Advisory Board meeting scheduled for the 26th, and Laposata's staff had their hands more than full. Thus, Commissioners Carey, Williams, and Foote would need to carry the football through in two back-to-back games.

Meeting with Parsons at the Pulaski Building on the eve of the two hearings, Williams and Kelley unveiled the Buckley renditions of the Rainbow Pool flanked by commemoration structures. Though still noncommittal, the park service associate director seemed to be warming toward Williams' preferred site.

J. Carter Brown called the morning hearing to order at the CFA headquarters. Williams would later regret that he had not personally engaged with Brown beforehand, since a deeper appreciation for this iconic Washingtonian would have reduced several hurdles. Brown, who would become one of Williams' staunchest allies, hailed from one of America's oldest families, with ancestors arriving in Rhode Island before 1630. Successful traders, the family built a textile factory in Pawtucket after the American Revolution, and the fortune this generated enabled them to endow a Providence college that now carries the family name. Brown's father, John Nicholas Brown, inherited and grew a family fortune that enabled him to study and collect art and pursue philanthropic endeavors. Serving in the Army during World War II as one of the "Monuments Men" charged with recovering stolen artworks from the Nazis, the senior Brown also served as President Truman's assistant secretary of the Navy.

J. Carter Brown inherited his father's interest in the arts as an undergraduate at Harvard and followed that up with a Harvard MBA. The younger Brown began his doctoral studies at the Institute of Fine Arts when he was lured to Washington in 1961 by an old family friend, John Walker, as the assistant director of the National Gallery of Art. In 1969, the thirty-four-year-old Brown succeeded Walker as director and made his mark on the nation's art scene. Described as part P. T. Barnum and part Albert Schweitzer, the aristocratic Brown was once dubbed "America's unofficial minister of culture" by *U.S. News and World Report*. During Brown's tenure as director, the National Art Gallery experienced tremendous growth, as exemplified by the addition of the I. M. Pei–designed East Wing of the gallery. Two years after landing the head job at the National Gallery, Brown was appointed by President Nixon to lead the Commission of Fine Arts. Stepping down from his National Gallery job in 1992 allowed Brown to focus on the CFA and his other civic duties. Chairing the CFA during the bicentennial years of the founding of the Republic provided Brown and his colleagues opportunities to make indelible marks on the capital landscape. One of the first challenges Brown faced during his tenure was the huge tract of property formerly occupied by Main Navy and the Munitions Buildings. Inspired by Olmsted, the CFA approved of a transformation to make the property Central Park-like, including a pond in the eastern section that was named Constitution Gardens.[26]

Looking up at Brown, Williams repeated his case for the Constitution Gardens site before the full commission. Brown thanked him and then asked to read three letters into the record. The first came from Sarah McClendon. The vice chair of the MAB site advice subcommittee offered her dissent on the ABMC primary choice, favoring instead property on Capitol grounds.

Following that blindside, Brown read the words of David Childs, the designer of Constitution Gardens, who observed that the memorial would ruin the park-like atmosphere. Finally, sculptor Frederick Hart suggested an alternative site, envisioning an Arc de Triomphe-type structure on the traffic circle on the opposite side of the Memorial Bridge, across the Potomac from the Lincoln Memorial.[27]

The Hart recommendation caught the attention of several of Brown's colleagues. CFA vice chairman Harold G. Robinson III liked the open vista along the river, and that the memorial could serve as a gateway to Arlington. Rex Ball noted that the traffic circle allowed for the vertical type of structure that many had envisioned for the Freedom Plaza site. Susan Rose joined in praise of Hart's concept. Brown then asked Ambassador Williams for his reaction. Caught off guard by Hart's recommendation, Williams countered that the veterans on his committee didn't want a drive-by memorial and preferred a site that could offer contemplation—something he saw was lacking in a traffic circle but certainly was present at the Rainbow Pool on the great axis of the Mall. Brown, who had previously made known his displeasure with the Constitution Gardens site, reminded Williams that the problem was that Constitution Gardens was *not* the Rainbow Pool but rather off to one side. He then stated that the Rainbow Pool site was a location that the CFA could support. Brown elaborated that people liked what they knew, and that both the Vietnam and Korean memorials were landscape solutions—something that could work at the Rainbow Pool. As for Constitution Gardens, Brown did not think the site was worthy of the event the ABMC sought to commemorate.[28]

Three pitches, three strikes, batter out. The Constitution Gardens option was not going to clear this hurdle—at least not at this time. During the ensuing discussions, Williams noted that Parsons did not react adversely when the subject of the Rainbow Pool site was brought up. At the end of the hearing, having rejected Site #4, Brown concluded that the Rainbow Pool could be a site worth considering, and also urged the ABMC to look across the Potomac at what was being called the "Columbia Island site."

Having failed to achieve their objectives before the first panel, the ABMC presenters regrouped and appeared before the National Capital Planning Commission, chaired by Harvey Gantt. In contrast to the aristocratic and privileged old-money Brown, Williams now looked up at an African American who had to sue to gain entry to Clemson University a year following Brown's arrival at the National Art Gallery. A U.S. Court of Appeals ruling forced Clemson to accept Gantt as its first black student on January 16, 1963, and three years later he graduated with honors with a degree in architecture. Furthering his education, Gantt attained a master's degree in city planning from MIT in 1970. Returning to the South, Gantt settled in Charlotte, North Carolina, where he co-launched a successful architectural firm that contributed to Charlotte's changing landscape during the 1970s and 1980s. Gantt also achieved success in politics, having been appointed in 1974 to the Charlotte City Council and then in 1983 became the city's first black mayor. In 1990, the popular Gantt ran statewide against the incumbent Senator Jesse Helms. Though defeated, his ability to attract 47 percent of the vote got him noticed at the National Democratic Party level, where he earned an invitation to come to Washington to serve on the Democratic National Committee. Unlike Brown, who had served in his post for more than two decades, Gantt had been with the NCPC for just over three months, having been appointed by President Clinton in April. Unlike the CFA, the NCPC, which had been founded in 1924, had a broader mandate to serve as the federal government's central planning agency for the capital and surrounding counties.

When Williams explained to Gantt the morning verdict, the new chair told the ambassador to go ahead and bring it on. So the Carey, Williams, and Foote trio gave an encore performance. Since John Parsons also had a seat on this commission, he also had the chance to weigh in, and actually submitted a motion to extend Site #4 to include the Rainbow Pool. Though the motion was shot down, Williams recognized he had won over the park service associate director. In the end, when Gantt called on his colleagues for a vote, the ABMC Constitution Gardens site request was approved just in time to allow

Carey, Williams, and Foote the opportunity to attend the Korean War Memorial dedication.

Now what? Ben Forgey reported the commissions' disconnect the next day in the *Washington Post*. Williams grabbed his pencil and legal pad to jot down options and concluded that the time had come to "go for broke on Rainbow Pool." On August 2, Williams called Buckley and then Atherton and reached a consensus on drafting a letter to the chairmen of the three commissions to seek a resolution. Sent out the following day, the letter generated a quick response from Parsons, who agreed to coordinate a conference call, since he alone remained in the nation's capital. Gantt had returned to his hometown of Charlotte, North Carolina; Brown was out in Sun Valley, Idaho; and Williams was visiting his sister at Duncans Mills in the Russian River Valley in Northern California.

The August 6 phone call achieved the breakthrough Williams had been hoping for. The quartet agreed that ABMC would evaluate the Columbia Island site (#7), along with any potential location along Memorial Drive leading to the entrance of Arlington Cemetery. More germane, the Rainbow Pool came into play as the new site # 8 candidate. The ABMC findings would then be presented to CFA and NCPC hearings scheduled for September.[29] Reflecting back two decades later, former commissioner Rolly Kidder observed, "I don't think you can understate the importance of the August 6th phone call between Williams, Brown, Parsons, and Gantt. Though it received no publicity and was 'off the record' so to speak—it not only broke the logjam over site decision, it also was the beginning of a very strong personal relationship between J. Carter Brown and Haydn Williams."[30]

After putting the substance of the understanding on paper for confirmation, Williams rushed back to San Francisco and boarded a plane back to the nation's capital to participate in an ABMC senior staff meeting on August 10. With summer temperatures in Washington, D.C., in the high nineties, the ambassador spent the next week networking, calling on Lieutenant General Kicklighter of the World War II Commemoration Committee, visiting with

Secretary Atherton, and visiting the White House to call on the president's counsel, Thomas "Mack" McLarty.

With the arrival of Labor Day marking the end of summer, the ABMC prepared for the upcoming hearings on September 19 before Brown's CFA panel, and then on October 5 before Gantt's group at the NCPC. For a change of pace, the ABMC World War II Memorial Committee converged in Boston on September 6 for a dinner meeting with General Woerner. Governor Carey, Ambassador Williams, and Brigadier General Foote felt confident that a positive outcome would soon be in hand. Two days later, Davis Buckley finalized the studies for sites #7 and #8, with a conclusion favoring the Rainbow Pool.[31]

Totally oblivious to the orchestrated moves by Williams that had abandoned the Constitution Gardens choice in favor of two new site selections, Sarah McClendon reached out to her MAB colleagues to dispel the notion that there was unanimity on Site #4 because she—for one—opposed it. She opened her September 13 letter by stating, "Dear Friends: I have done a lot of investigating lately about the World War II Memorial." What McClendon uncovered, which was no longer germane to the situation at hand, was that David Henley of the Thomas Paine Memorial Foundation believed he had the support of John Parsons to place its proposed memorial at 1776 Constitution Avenue—which happened to be on the grounds of the Constitution Gardens. Parsons told McClendon he didn't think he made a commitment but Henley "has been giving him lots of trouble." Citing this as one of several reasons to steer clear of the Constitution Gardens site, McClendon also expressed concern that site limitations might also preempt a designer's ability to build interior educational and exhibition spaces. In restating her case for a Mall location near the Capitol building, McClendon concluded with a prescient observation, "We made a mistake by not discussing form, design, size, and purpose before picking site."[32]

As McClendon sent off her missive, Williams flew back into the nation's capital to meet with Buckley on September 14, to go over conceptual drawings for the Columbia Island and Rainbow Pool sites. The next day they called on J. Carter Brown to give him a preview of the drawings and seek any helpful tips for the upcoming presentation on the 19th. Clearly, the rapport that had developed since the failed July 27 hearing shaped the much more collegial September meeting. Showing appropriate humility, Williams read from his thirteen-page prepared statement: "We now have a site recommendation that is far better for having been reshaped and honed by questions, suggestions, and criticisms." Now arguing for the location that he had set his eyes on at the start of the year, the ambassador had difficulty containing his enthusiasm as he gushed on about the central Mall location, concluding that the Rainbow Pool site was "commensurate with the importance and impact of World War II on the life of America and the world."

During the ensuing discussion, CFA vice chairman Harold G. Robinson III read a prepared statement lauding the symbolism and spirit of the site as fitting. Williams jotted down: "Very, very well written and can be useful." However, the vice chair also cautioned the ABMC petitioners to consult with the CFA on the yet-to-be-selected design, expressing concern about the stately elm trees that flanked the north and south ends of Olmsted's pool. Brown echoed Robinson's caution. The comments proved only cautionary, for after a short deliberation, the CFA voted unanimously for the Rainbow Pool site to host the World War II Memorial.[33]

As Ben Forgey reported news of the Tuesday CFA decision in Wednesday's *Washington Post*, Williams prepared for his Thursday meeting with Harvey Gantt to discuss the forthcoming NCPC hearing on October 5. In addition to looking ahead at jumping the next immediate hurdle, Williams saw the need for better ABMC and MAB coordination, because the design phase of the project could now be seen on the horizon. No need for freelancing reporters. Thus, on September 29, General Woerner and Chairman Wheeler signed a revised ABMC-MAB memorandum of understanding, which featured a new paragraph 6 on the responsibilities and activities of the ABMC Memorial Committee (soon to be rebranded as the Site and Design Committee). Ambassador Williams would serve as the chair, since Governor Carey intended to step away from the ABMC to tend to other obligations. However, the Empire State would still be represented by commissioner Rolland Kidder, who would be assigned to join with Williams and Foote. Helen Fagin from the MAB would be the new board liaison.

Kidder's placement on the team seemed preordained, given the interest he had shown in the memorial project starting back when Williams had first mentioned it to him in Italy. Unlike the Brooklyn-born Carey, Kidder hailed from Jamestown in the western part of the state. Graduating from Houghton College, Kidder earned a commission in the U.S. Navy and served on river patrol boats (PBRs) in the Mekong Delta between 1969 and 1970. The combat veteran subsequently earned a law degree and served four terms in the state assembly as a Democrat representing his hometown's district during Hugh Carey's time in Albany. An entrepreneur, Kidder founded a natural gas exploration company that enabled him to continue supporting his party long after he left elective office. Whether it was the common naval service legacy or the tremendous patriotic love both men shared for country, Williams and Kidder, despite party differences, were kindred spirits.[34]

Once again, the ABMC presentation team appeared before the NCPC and gave a pitch similar to that heard by the CFA. In addition to the unanimous earlier verdict rendered by the CFA, a strong letter of support for the Rainbow Pool site from National Park Service director Robert G. Stanton impressed the dozen-member commission. However, not everyone was sold. As one of the District of Columbia's representatives on the panel, Pat Elwood voiced reservations "about the ability of any design not to impact this spacious grandeur." Leery of an unknown future design, Elwood warned her colleagues that, once they committed to the site, "it is really hard to draw back." Two of her colleagues joined her in voting against the proposed siting. The next day Ben Forgey's *Washington Post* banner read: "WWII Memorial gets Choice Mall Site—Second Panel Approves Location, Clearing Way for Design Phase."[35]

While the newsprint with the celebratory headline was just hours old, Williams convened his Site and Design Committee together to discuss what

to do next. Spurred on by comments made by one of the NCPC commissioners, the new committee tracked out a timeline that envisioned completion of
the memorial in 2000. But before the memorial could be built, it needed to
be designed.

Chapter Three

THE NATIONAL DESIGN COMPETITION

1996

ETERANS DAY, 1995: The overcast skies and occasional cold showers reminded Rolly Kidder of a similar day eleven months earlier, when he and Pat Foote had walked with Haydn Williams past the Rainbow Pool and heard him opine that this would be a fitting location for the World War II Memorial. Today that vision would take another step toward reality as the president, whose father had fought in the Italian campaign, arrived to dedicate the site. This was the closing event of a series of commemorations marking the fiftieth anniversary of the war's end. Each event marked a pivotal point of World War II, starting with the attack on Pearl Harbor all the way to the Japanese surrender in Tokyo Bay. Of course, the commissioners all had taken part in the grandest of the commemorations a year earlier, when they overlooked the beaches of Normandy.

In contrast to the D-Day commemoration, this ceremony was relatively low-key, with about five hundred attendees. Kidder recalled, "It looked as if it had been thrown together—the platform was low, the PA system wasn't very strong, and I didn't see a lot of press." The ceremony lasted about an hour.

Following the introduction of the official party and the national anthem and invocation, Governor Carey stepped up to the podium to welcome the guests. He spoke of his experience as an Army infantry officer in the fight for northern France and how that experience shaped him through a remarkably successful political career. Chairman Peter Wheeler of the Memorial Advisory Board offered his welcome and introduced Congresswoman Marcy Kaptur, who reminded those in attendance about the significance of the war and her efforts to shepherd the necessary legislation that made that day's event possible. She was followed by Helen Boyajian, a former parachute seamstress from Lowell, Massachusetts, who discussed the strong support for the war effort on the home front. Following an introduction by the chairman of the Joint Chiefs of Staff, Gen. John Shalikashvili, and then Dr. Miguel Encinias, President Clinton stepped up to the podium. Always the polished speaker, the president again delivered poignant words to mark the occasion: "If they could serve as brothers abroad, they could live as neighbors at home. . . . [T]his memorial would commemorate a generation who had changed the course of American life and the direction of world history."[1]

A veteran of the Tenth Armored Division that served as a component of Gen. George Patton's Third Army proved to be the star attraction. Roger Durbin, who experienced some of the most vicious combat during the Battle of the Bulge, was acknowledged by all of the speakers and praised by the president, who thanked the Ohioan "for his idea and for the triumph of the idea today, and the triumph of the idea that an American citizen can have a good idea and take it to the proper authorities and actually get something done." After the president's remarks, Durbin was invited to join with President Clinton to unveil a plaque marking the nation's commitment to build a memorial at that site. Durbin also joined with the president and a dozen other dignitaries (including four representatives each from the ABMC and MAB) to consecrate the site with soil that had been collected from fourteen overseas ABMC World War II cemeteries, plus the Veterans Administration's National Memorial Cemetery of the Pacific on Oahu (the Punchbowl).[2]

With the marker now in place, the ABMC could refocus on preparing for the two immediate challenges ahead—determining just what was going to be built at the Rainbow Pool site and funding the project. The two objectives were related in that producing a visual concept of the end product would certainly spur contributions. However, even without having a memorial design to show-case, there were some internal challenges to overcome. The MAB had commis-sioned a fundraising consultant to test the waters for a major capital campaign and reported back that "the receptivity to funding appeals not as strong as had been hoped." The best could be hoped for was $35 million. The challenge proved a bit much for Moorhead, who stepped down as the chair of the MAB fundraising committee. In addition, another leadership void occurred when Lieutenant General Laposata stepped down as the ABMC secretary.[3]

To find that candidate to replace Laposata, ABMC executive director Ken Pond knew of an individual with whom he had served in the Army and for whom he had great respect. With retirement looming, Maj. Gen. John P. Herrling, who commanded the U.S. Army Training Center at Fort Dix, New Jersey, received a call from Pond advising him that the position was open and that he should consider it. Having interviewed other candidates, Woerner set-tled on Herrling. The general was a product of the Finger Lakes region of New York State who attended the University of Scranton and earned a commission as an Army second lieutenant through that school's ROTC program. Entering the service in the 1960s as an infantry officer, Herrling served two tours in Vietnam with the 101st Airborne Division and advised a Vietnamese air-borne brigade. On his second tour, he earned a Purple Heart after fragments of a mortar shell injured him and killed two of his fellow soldiers. He rose through the ranks over a thirty-five-year career that led to a final tour at Fort Dix. General Woerner would later acknowledge his hiring of Herrling to fill Laposata's boots as one of his more significant accomplishments.[4]

Herrling became acquainted with the ABMC staff at the antiquated Pulaski Building, put out a hiring notice for a professional fundraiser, and began the interviewing process. Meanwhile, Haydn Williams, MAB member

Helen Fagin, and fellow commissioners Doug Kinnard and Hugh Carey met with ABMC consulting architect Paul Cret Harbeson two days before the site dedication ceremony at the Holiday Inn in Old Town Alexandria.[5] As the discussion about a design competition progressed, Williams jotted down items to specify in a competition announcement. This announcement would include a program statement, site constraints and sensitivities, the review timeline, procedural questions, and germane federal regulations.[6]

Another question that needed to be addressed was: who would manage the project from the standpoint of announcing the design competition and contracting to build the selected design? The ABMC had experience with the Army Corps of Engineers, with the recently dedicated Korean War Memorial. However, Harbeson steered Williams in a different direction. When Williams arrived in Washington in December 1995, they met with Marilyn Farley of the General Services Administration (GSA). Williams was most impressed with GSA's Design Excellence program, which had been proven for federal construction projects. In further discussions at the December 18 Site and Design Committee meeting, Harbeson and Colonel Kelley presented the pros and cons of an open versus limited competition. Open competitions had produced the winning designs for the Vietnam and the Korean War Veterans Memorials, but they had been tedious processes and, in the case of the Korean War Veterans Memorial, led to court actions by the designers against the Korean War Memorial Advisory Board. In contrast, the ABMC had a history of sending out proposal requests for designs to well-established firms, which resulted in many of the magnificent structures associated with its overseas cemeteries. The committee decided that the competition needed to be somewhere in between. The ABMC consultant and staffer also anticipated that the process would involve several stages. Kidder remembered that Williams favored a more limited selection process: "A national competition would take more time and delay the memorial's construction."[7]

As the calendar changed to the presidential election year of 1996, Senator Bob Dole spent much of his time campaigning in Iowa, with a goal of winning the caucuses of that state on February 12. Overcoming a Pat Buchanan victory in the New Hampshire primary, the popular Kansas senator would cruise to a Republican Party nomination to face President Clinton in the fall election.

With the last World War II veteran ever to make a run for the White House engaged in his campaign, the effort to honor him and the remaining millions who served in that great conflict continued in the nation's capital. Four days into the new year, a joint meeting was held between the new MAB Public Relations and Fundraising Committee and the ABMC World War II Site and Design Committee. Colonel Kelley reported that the project account had nearly 9.5 million dollars, of which half had come from coin sales. A little more than $800,000 had been contracted out to cover the costs of consultants such as Davis Buckley, purchasing the fundraising software, the dedication ceremony, and travel expenses. With a projected budget now set at $110 million, a fundraising counsel had assembled a spiral bound *WWII Memorial Capital Campaign* playbook. As Williams studied the pages of the fundraising planning document, he came across the case statement for the memorial and zeroed in on this sentence: "The concept of a 'just war'—a war fought for justice, freedom, and liberation—has faded from our vocabulary in recent years." Having resided in one of the centers of protest against the war in Vietnam, Williams underlined the next line with his marker: "World War II was a just war. We need to remind our children of that!"

The playbook offered a dual-track strategy to engage individuals through a marketing campaign and direct mail solicitation. Organizational donations from veterans' groups, nonprofit organizations, and corporate support would also be tapped. National in scope, the playbook recommended six geographical mini regions. Williams underlined the expectation that Congress would contribute toward half of the goal with a $10-million-dollar earmark appropriated for the next five years. Recommendations that would be accepted included the hiring of a major public relations firm and a strong campaign coordinator.[8]

Since the SDC, now led by Williams, was to meet at the end of January, agreement was reached on a process. First, candidates would be vetted to meet a list of predetermined qualifications. Once they were vetted, the submissions entered would be screened by an ABMC-assembled panel with representatives from the public and private sectors. Once the entries were whittled down to six, a GSA-recommended blind jury would join in on the final judging process.[9] Reviewing the minutes of the meeting where the projected announcement date would be March 1, Williams wrote, "Questionable."

The ambassador returned to Washington for a series of meetings on February 8 and 9. One accomplishment Williams facilitated was a revised memorandum of understanding between the ABMC and the MAB to establish a ten-person joint campaign and policy committee. This was to be chaired by Jess Hay, who was well qualified thanks to a pedigree that included a stint as finance chair of the Democratic Party. Commissioners Carey, Foote, Kidder, Williams, and the recently appointed Ed Romero represented the ABMC. Besides Hay, MAB representation consisted of Roger Durbin's granddaughter Melissa Durbin, Miguel Encinias, Jon Mangis, and Bill Murphy. Another joint committee was formed to work the Hill for federal funding, with Ed Romero and Thomas G. Lyons of the ABMC and Jess Hay and J. William Murphy of the MAB.[10]

With the structural modifications earning the approval signatures of Chairman Wheeler and General Woerner, the joint campaign and policy committee held its inaugural meeting. Jess Hay reported on efforts to recruit former presidents as honorary campaign chairs. As for a potential national chairman, Hay had reached out to Coca Cola CEO Roberto Goizueta but had not heard back. Regarding the announcement of the national design competition, Williams noted that the target date was now March 15, though he expected that would also slip. He reminded his colleagues that in his mind, the announcement represented a point of no return for the campaign.[11]

During the following day, Williams attended the ABMC Executive Committee meeting and shared the philosophy that was shaping the design program. Working with Paul Harbeson and the GSA, the SDC wrestled with the following questions in shaping design specifications: (1) How much freedom should be offered to designers? (2) How proscriptive should the guidelines be? and (3) What about the educational element?[12]

Over the next two weeks, faxes shot forth and back between Washington and San Francisco as the ABMC refined the announcement specifications. Williams jotted down on his yellow legal pad: "Do it right from the start." Returning to Washington for a February 29 SDC meeting, Ambassador Williams consulted with Colonel Kelley to confirm that the GSA should act as ABMC's agent and administer the national design competition. The Army Corps of Engineers under GSA direction would oversee the actual construction. The new ABMC secretary, Major General Herrling, reported that he was crafting the necessary memorandums of agreement between the federal agencies. Speaking to the *Washington Post* later, Williams recalled, "We had looked very carefully at the experiences of the Vietnam Veterans Memorial and the Korean Veterans Memorial."[13] As a result, in contrast to the Vietnam and Korean memorials' design competitions, which had been open to all competitors, the SDC desired to identify entrants "through a careful professional selection process who have the greatest promise as designers" during the first stage of the competition: "The goal is to encourage competition, to make Stage 1 as open as possible within the limits of practicality. Limits—Winner must be a U.S. citizen and the design firm must be U.S."[14]

The "careful professional selection process" was defined in selection criteria that scored 50 percent just on the company's past performance and the lead designer's résumé. In a briefing memorandum to the MAB at the end of March, Kelley stated that the design specifications called for a strong educational component; however, that an aboveground education center might not meet with the approval of one of the three oversight commissions. Kelley anticipated an underground facility somewhat modeled on the Sackler Museum. In conclusion, Kelley observed that the SDC felt that a visit to the World War II Memorial should be an "educational, inspiring, and uplifting experience, certainly not in the sense of glorifying war, but as a reminder to future American generations of the climactic event of the 20th century, a time when our country was united in a common cause, and the significance of World War II on subsequent American and world history."[15]

The vehicle used by the ABMC and GSA to announce the competition was the *Commerce Business Daily*, which posted the design specifications in its April 19 edition. GSA also posted the announcement on this relatively new digital outlet called the Internet. The due date for the submission would be June 17, 1996.[16]

Unfortunately for the ABMC and the GSA, the judging criteria set in the competition specifications made it apparent that young—potentially very creative—upstart designers without an established portfolio need not apply. Candidates such as Maya Lin, the twenty-one-year-old Yale undergraduate student who beat out 1,421 other submissions for the Vietnam Veterans Memorial, would be shunned.

Paul Spreiregen, who consulted on the competition that had selected the Lin design, best articulated the reaction within the architectural community in a May 5 *Washington Post* op-ed piece titled "A Democratic Approach For Our World War II Memorial." He argued that the selection criteria were "exclusionary, cumbersome, restrictive, arbitrary, and—worst of all for the subject at hand—[an] undemocratic process." Instead, based on his experience with the Vietnam Veterans Memorial, Spreiregen offered an alternative two-stage competition process that wasn't exclusionary.[17]

Feedback from Spreiregen and others was noted. On May 17, the ABMC and GSA revised the selection criteria so that past design performance was weighted 10 percent less, adding 10 percent to the lead designer's vision. They also extended the submission date out to July 15. Three days later, a pre-submission meeting hosted by GSA chief architect Ed Feiner at GSA headquarters to allow potential entrants to ask questions, turned into a confrontational forum as a group of students based at the local Virginia Tech Washington-Alexandria Architectural Consortium came to have their voices heard. Furthermore, the director of the consortium, Jaan Holt, came with a petition signed by deans of architecture programs located in fourteen states.

Despite Feiner's contention that the revised criteria would allow for that "diamond-in-the-rough," the students argued that the revised criteria still eliminated students, interns, and other independent practitioners. Benjamin Forgey's summation in the next day's *Washington Post*, under the headline "War Memorial Battle," portended some heavy seas ahead if the ABMC-GSA maintained the current course.[18]

Undoubtedly, Williams saw the Forgey piece that morning as he prepared for the next meeting of the SDC. Concerned that the design selection controversy could impinge on fundraising, Williams welcomed the offer to have William "Bill" Lacy serve as a consultant to shepherd a new competition announcement. The former president of Cooper Union, then president of the State University of New York at Purchase, provided the ABMC-GSA partnership with instant credibility. Besides also previously directing the architecture and design program at the National Endowment of the Arts for seven years, more germane to the task at hand was that Lacy was currently serving as the executive director of the Chicago-based Pritzker Architecture Prize. This was considered to be one of the world's most prestigious honors in the profession, with the annual winning architect(s) receiving a bronze medallion and $100,000 in prize money. Suspecting that J. Carter Brown had a role in the recruitment, Rolly Kidder approved the move to get Lacy as "he had the bonafides."[19]

At the May 21 SDC meeting, Williams agreed to Lacy's proposal to start the competition afresh, with a call to welcome entrants without established portfolios or major design firm affiliation. Over the next three weeks, the two men chatted by phone and exchanged faxes to wordsmith the new announcement. On June 6, Lacy responded to Williams' latest series of edits to say the new announcement would address the "legitimate concerns expressed at the pre-submittal meeting on May 20, 1996. This intensive review has resulted, I believe, in a document which you and your committee should be able to approve in confidence."[20]

The letter arrived in time for consideration at the next day's SDC meeting. The committee approved the new call for design submissions. Less than a week later, the new announcement had been made, with a new due date of August 13. In a GSA press release, Major General Herrling stated, "The structure of this open competition and selection process is designed to ensure the widest possible participation. There is no entry fee, and the only requirements are that the designer be over eighteen years of age and a U.S. citizen."[21]

Not many architects subscribe to the *Commerce Business Daily* or look for GSA press releases, but during the 1990s they would receive their monthly edition of *Architecture*. When the July edition of that journal arrived at a boutique three-person firm in Providence, Rhode Island, the firm's lead architect took note of journal editor Deborah Dietsch's scornful overview of plans for a World War II memorial. Opening her editorial by expressing hope that the "atrocious new Korean War Veterans Memorial would be the last war memorial on the Mall," Dietsch summarized the design competition process and expressed concern that the Rainbow Pool was ill-suited as a site: "Only an unmonumental monument—low, limited, and landscaped—seems appropriate for this symbolic axis. But such deference is at odds with the purpose of this war memorial: to remind Americans of one of the World's most colossal conflicts. It will take a genius indeed to solve this dilemma and preserve the Mall's vista."[22]

In Providence, a boutique architect welcomed the challenge.[23]

With the successful reboot of the design competition, the SDC turned to the next agenda item—the process for judging a winner. Under Lacy's guiding hand, the revised path forward would involve an evaluation panel to screen the entry concepts and whittle them down to six, and then an independent design jury to select a winning entry from the finalists, alongside a pick from the evaluation panel. Calls had been sent out to the ABMC commissioners and MAB members to offer candidates for Lacy to assemble for selection at the next SDC.

Meeting three days before the nation's 220th birthday, the SDC reviewed names that Lacy had compiled over the previous month and placed into various categories. These included architectural engineers, landscape architects, art curators, art critics, journalists, military members—especially World War II veterans, as well as historians. As Lacy briefed the committee about the backgrounds of the candidates, Williams crossed out some names and circled others, in some cases adding exclamation points (!!!). The MAB liaison to the committee, Helen Fagin, made her notations, as did Pat Foote. (Foote was now performing her chores as a commissioner while again serving on active duty; she had been recalled to serve a one-year stint as a vice chair on an Army panel reviewing sexual harassment in the service.) Commissioner Rolly Kidder, now a permanent member of the committee occupying the spot once occupied by Governor Carey, who had left the commission earlier in the year, also evaluated the choices.[24] With the choices made, Lacy was then delegated to contact the desired dozen who would form the so-called Architect-Engineer Evaluation Board. So-called because, as previously noted, the panel would be inclusive of historians, journalists, and military veterans.

Two individuals Lacy did not have to track down were Haydn Williams, who volunteered to represent the ABMC, and Ed Feiner, the chief architect of the GSA. Noted New York architect Hugh Hardy would chair the board, to be joined by fellow New York architect J. Max Bond Jr. and Cynthia Weese of Washington University in St. Louis. Mary Margaret Jones of San Francisco offered her expertise as a landscape architect, as did Pulitzer Prize–winning architecture critic of the *Boston Globe* Robert Campbell. Military representation included former Marine Corps commandant Gen. Louis H. Wilson; Col. Mary Hallaren, who once commanded the Women's Army Corps, and former Tuskegee Airman Luther Smith. Eminent military historian Russell F. Weigley rounded out the board.[25]

When the deadline date for submissions arrived on August 13, Bill Lacy tallied 406 entrants. Most members of the evaluation board arrived in Washington for the judging on August 15 and 16. Lacy had made arrangements to borrow a fitting space to hang the 20 x 20–inch concept sketches—the ground floor of the great hall of the Pension Building, which had recently been repurposed to become the National Building Museum. The concept sketches, mounted on extended rows of portable panels, had no outward entrant identification, because the submitters were instructed to insert their identification in a sealed envelope taped to the back of the foam core board backing. The board worked their way through the aisles three times that first day, quickly eliminating a majority of the concepts during the first two passes. Hugh Hardy recalled, "We began by eliminating what we thought was inappropriate to what essentially is there—a place of contemplation." Hardy noted that many of the entrants had submitted designs for what he classified as a battle monument: "A battle monument is very specific and is usually about individual heroism." Instead, Hardy expressed interest in submissions that complemented the Washington and Lincoln Memorials with "involved ideas of much larger scope."[26]

Hardy and his cohorts quickly eliminated innovative concepts that required machinery to facilitate motion as long-term maintenance nightmares. Glass and polished metal entrants drew similar concern about durability. Williams recalled the predominance of eagles in many of the designs. As the board cut one of the eagle designs from contention, Williams observed, "Well, there goes another eagle," to which General Wilson retorted, "Yes, but there are still quite a lot of turkeys left." During the final walkthrough on the 15th to narrow the field to twenty-five candidates, the cuts became more difficult.[27]

The next day the evaluation board went back to work to whittle down the twenty-five remaining concepts to six. "We were looking for variety in the finalists' list," recounted Hardy. At the end of the day, the verdict was rendered.[28]

"Designs on History: Finalists Chosen for World War II Memorial" read the clever headline Benjamin Forgey's report in the August 22 edition of the *Washington Post*. In his story, Forgey reported that each of the six finalists would receive $75,000 to spend over the next two months, to flesh out their concept into a more concrete design. Not published in the article were any images of the finalist concepts. Lacy explained, "At this stage I think it would be wrong for each of the entrants to view what the others had done."[29]

The six finalists were notified and brought to Washington. For Lacy, the diversified backgrounds of the entrants affirmed that the process had been democratized. Finalists included Princeton graduate students, a Yale professor, a former dean of architecture at the Rhode Island School of Design who now ran a boutique firm, the head of a world-renowned architectural firm, partners who had previously designed the Women's Memorial and Education Center over at Arlington Cemetery, and a pair of local architects affiliated with the world's fourth-largest design firm.[30]

The finalists had an inkling on what to expect, thanks to the posting made in the August 23 *Commerce Business Daily* of the program for the second stage of the competition. The new guidance repeated the requirement that the new structure blend in with the local environment and maintain the east-west vista. Adding to the challenge was the ABMC requirement for 7,400 square meters of interior space for exhibitions and ceremonies. The final evaluation criteria would also be re-promulgated—past experience and professional qualifications would be factored in.[31]

At the August 29 gathering, Lacy took time to interview each of the entrants, to go over the ground rules and answer any questions on the remaining stage of the competition. Williams sat in on the conversations. One of the entrants appeared nervous, perhaps believing that they would mistake him for a noncitizen because of his foreign accent and thus disqualify him. Williams watched in fascination as the Austrian-born Friedrich St.Florian fumbled to needlessly pull his passport out of his pant pocket to assure Lacy that he was a legitimate U.S. citizen.[32]

With the finalists gathered together, Williams took a moment to share his passion about the project: "What you will be designing will symbolize and memorialize a moment in time which, in profound ways, changed forever the face of American life and the direction of world history."[33]

Having received their marching orders, the finalists went back to their respective drawing boards to produce seven 30 x 40-inch wide depictions offering various perspectives of how they would develop the site. For Williams and the SDC, the two-month period preparing for the final selection brought on additional chores to tackle. First, in addition to reconvening the Architect-Engineer

Evaluation Board in late October, the ABMC-GSA process called for a design jury. Another noted New York architect, David Childs, was chosen to lead the jury. Childs, who had designed the nearby Constitution Gardens site, knew the lay of the land. He would be joined by the aforementioned Hugh Hardy, Houston architect John S. Chase, San Francisco architect Cathy J. Simon, landscape architect Laurie Olin, architectural critic Ada Louise Huxtable, National Gallery of Art director Earl A. Powell III, PepsiCo chairman and CEO (and World War II veteran) Donald M. Kendall, and to represent the military, retired Adm. Robert L. Long, and Gen. John W. Vessey Jr. GSA chief architect Feiner, ABMC consultant architect Harbeson, and Ambassador Williams would serve as advisers to the jury.[34]

With a project timeline that initially proposed a final memorial dedication sometime in 2000, the fundraising aspect of the project assumed greater priority during the national election, where the two major political parties were vying for public attention and contributions. With the design competition hiccups smoothed over, the capital campaign organization matured with the hiring of Jay Hadley as the campaign director and Col. Joe Purka, USAF (Ret.), as the director of public relations. Another retired Air Force colonel, Mike Conley, joined the growing team to serve as Colonel Purka's deputy. Other members of the staff and MAB ventured out to the summer conventions of the American Legion and the Veterans of Foreign Wars (VFW) to whip up support. As the number of contributors began to grow, Colonel Purka sent out the first World War II Memorial newsletter to inform donors about the ongoing design competition. On the negative side, the MAB committee targeting Capitol Hill for federal support made little headway. Overall, staffing requirements were such that they needed additional office space in the venerable Pulaski Building. Beginning on October 1, ABMC would not only occupy the entire fifth floor, but also take on office space on the first floor.[35]

When Williams convened a meeting of the SDC in mid-September to review the details of the selection process slated for the end of October, an add-on to the discussion was the latest in a spate of critical pieces written by architects or architectural critics that had some contention with the site location or the design expectations.[36] Forgey's recent *Washington Post* piece, "Tactical Error: World War II Monument Site Is No Place For Museum," published a week prior to the SDC conclave, argued that the need for so much interior space on a Mall location was inappropriate. Reviewing the negative commentary, the committee decided not to let this shot across the bow go unanswered. Over the next week, facsimile machines on the East and West Coasts poured out paper as Williams' handwritten words were typed and returned for editing and rewriting. In his September 29 *Washington Post* op-ed rejoinder titled "The Right Place for a Memorial," Williams clarified that while the ABMC sought interior space, there was "a misunderstanding of our intentions" about placing a museum at the site with requirements for a curator and permanent staff. Published as the design competition entered its final month, the Williams counter-commentary provided additional guidance to the six finalist design teams.[37]

October 1996 would be marked as a month of competition as President Bill Clinton and his Republican opponent Robert Dole stumped the nation seeking votes for a national election to be held on November 5. A day later, the SDC would meet to consider the recommendations of the Architect-Engineer Evaluation Board and the recently convened design jury. Though there seemed to be no correlation between the two contests at the time, in retrospect, the reelection of the president would have positive consequences for the World War II Memorial project, for it assured continuity within the ABMC for the next four years and made available an individual who would serve as a most worthy champion.

The President's Guest House, known as Blair House, had served as the judging venue for the Childs-led jury. Across Pennsylvania Avenue from the northwest side of the executive mansion, the complex consisted of four former nineteenth-century residences centered on an 1824 vintage home, which had been acquired by Francis Preston Blair and had remained in the family for over a century. The residence of Harry and Bess Truman during an extensive White

House refurbishment, the facility offered ample meeting rooms for the six finalists to display and explain their concepts.

Thanks to the efforts of Marilyn Farley, who arranged for this exquisite GSA-managed property to be made available, the design jury met at Blair House for the first time over breakfast on the morning of October 29, having first toured the Rainbow Pool site before beginning their deliberations. The panel reviewed renderings submitted by three of the entrants in a morning session, and after lunch discussed the merits of the drawings submitted by the other three contestants. On the next day, the Architect-Engineer Evaluation Board reconvened at GSA headquarters and evaluated the submitted drawings. The board also spent an hour with each competing team for a presentation and a question-and-answer session, and then rendered their own verdict.[38]

An argument can be made that, in selecting six contrasting design concepts for consideration, the evaluation board had unknowingly given an edge to the design most closely correlating to what Davis Buckley had crafted for Williams a year earlier, to impress John Parsons of the National Park Service. Upon seeing the winning design, J. Carter Brown stated, "It has a certain inevitability that I think is quite inspiring."[39]

An educational/exhibition space comparable to what had been installed with the recently completed Women's Military Memorial in Arlington and the Navy Memorial on Pennsylvania Avenue also proved to be a challenge. Given the design constraints, five of the design teams offered a subterranean solution for the interior space.

The following concepts were extracted from a GSA booklet published at the time of the World War II Memorial's dedication. From Marion Weiss and Michael A. Manfredi's entry from their New York studios came "Light Columns."[40]

A grid of 50 crystalline columns of light stand together in the Rainbow Pool, representing the collective efforts of the nation united together in a common and just cause at home and abroad. An east-west below-ground ramp on the centerline of the Mall under the Rainbow Pool forms a timeline of the war. Starting on the east side of the Rainbow Pool, a slow descent marks each year of the inconceivable destruction of the war abroad. The depth of the descent reflects the magnitude of the tragedy engulfing the world beyond the boundaries of America. Directly below the Rainbow Pool marks America's entry into the darkness of World War II. It is an underground Hall of Honor defined by the shadow and light from the columns above in the pool. The steep ascent, with its view west toward the Lincoln Memorial, marks the end of the war and the return to peace.

Another New York entry came from Rafael Viñoly.[41] The immigrant from Uruguay, who attained architectural acclaim in his homeland, had come to New York in the 1970s to build on his reputation. He offered "The Light of Memory."

The heart of the memorial is the Hall of Remembrance, a circular room symbolizing unity, sunken beneath the Rainbow Pool. Open to the sky, the hall is constantly transformed by the ever-changing light and shadows that filter through from an eternal ring of fire and cascading water above that forms a colored mist in the center of the pool. The geometry of the Rainbow Pool remains intact but is expanded with two peripheral fan-shaped pools on the north and south representing the Atlantic and Pacific Oceans. The semicircular edges of these pools are framed by the two peristyles of monolithic triangular glass prisms that refract natural light and produce rainbow patterns, which extend into the landscape. The colors, and their changing reflections, express the hope secured in victory.

Roger Durbin's question to Congresswoman Marcy Kaptur in February 1987 inspired the World War II Memorial, and the rest is history as they championed this issue through the corridors of power in Washington, D.C., with leaders of both parties. *Courtesy of Congresswoman Marcy Kaptur*

Lt. (jg) F. Haydn Williams.
Courtesy of Friends of the National World War II Memorial

J. Carter Brown (*center*) and the Commission of Fine Arts, meeting circa 1998.
Courtesy of Commission of Fine Arts

The Site and Design Committee meeting at Leo A. Daly. *Courtesy of Friends of the National World War II Memorial*

SDC members Frank Moore, Pat Foote, Helen Fagin, Haydn Williams, and Rolly Kidder with a model of the memorial. *Courtesy of Friends of the National World War II Memorial*

President Bill Clinton surrounded by Pat Foote, Frank Moore, Haydn Williams, Rolly Kidder, and Marcy Kaptur. *Courtesy of Friends of the National World War II Memorial*

President George W. Bush signs the National World War II Memorial Bill, allowing construction of the World War II Memorial to proceed. *Courtesy of Friends of the National World War II Memorial*

A hardhat salute! *Courtesy of Friends of the National World War II Memorial*

Senator Bob Dole speaking at the World War II Memorial Dedication Ceremony. *Don Ripper (Latoff Inc.) / American Battle Monuments Commission*

Haydn Williams next to a wreath at the World War II Memorial. *Courtesy of Friends of the National World War II Memorial.*

A local entry came from Bernard J. Wulff and William C. Jackson, of the Washington offices of the global RTKL Associates architectural firm, offering "The Bell Garden." [42]

> The elements of sound, landscape, and water are joined to create a restrained and reverent place. A colonnade composed of two semi-circular structures supporting 192 bells in clusters of 48 are set in the existing trees and garden areas on the north and south sides of the Rainbow Pool. The Rainbow Pool is rebuilt of honed black granite covered with a thin layer of clear, filtered water to create a mirror-like surface that reflects the surroundings. The plaza is paved in white granite and is framed by two semicircular seating walls that define the garden areas. The bell garden is a place of quiet contemplation. The soft tolling of the bells and reflections in the pool are designed to evoke boundless memories and aspirations of a people joined together in the cause of freedom—then, now, and in the future. "Let freedom ring."

A fourth entry came from Brian M. Ambroziak, a graduate student at Princeton University. It was titled "The Bunker."[43]

> Implementing the formal strategy of the 1901 McMillan Plan for the Mall, this memorial is a grand avenue forming a north-south cross axis between the Reflecting Pool and the Rainbow Pool that leaves open the vista between the Lincoln Memorial and the Washington Monument. The memorial is primarily a subterranean structure that eliminates large aboveground elements and preserves the graceful row of elm trees. Above ground, the symbolic forms used are derived from the architecture of the war. The primary iconic element is the bunker. Removed from the theater of war, the bunker confronts the observer as an anachronism, a muted structure of

survival now displaced to an era of stability and strength. The bunker is meant to give voice to many elements that shaped Americans' battle for personal survival and global redemption. As such it represents a historic milestone.

The entry from landscape architect Diana Balmori, from New Haven, Connecticut, would have removed the oval-shaped Olmsted Rainbow Pool in favor of a square one, in a design that was titled "Island and Cube of Time and Space."[44]

In this scheme, a rectangular reflective pool of black granite and jets of white water replace the Rainbow Pool with a glowing alabaster cube-shaped platform at the surface in the center. The platform is a luminescent ceiling for an alabaster Hall of Honor below ground. An east-west walkway on the centerline of the Mall forms an axis of Time—1931, 1936, 1941, 1945—across the center of the island, while a north-south ramp under the center of the island leads to an underground hall and forms an axis of Space representing Europe, Asia, Africa, and America. Together, these axes weave World War II into one continuous cloth forming a memorial of memory in motion.

For Laurie Olin and others on the jury who savored contemporary designs, the Balmori concept had immense appeal. However, at the end of the day the design jury selected "The Forum" concept submitted by Friedrich St.Florian, the former dean of architecture and design at the Rhode Island School of Design. St.Florian's concept read,

The existing Rainbow Pool and surrounding plaza are lowered 15 feet to create an enclosed, meditative space. Two semicircular earthen berms, 33 feet tall and 90 feet wide, [are] covered in a carpet of white roses form a north-south axis that encloses the memorial

precinct and provides exhibition space. Semicircular colonnades—
consisting of 50 abstract columns, each representing a state—frames
the interior of the berms, symbolizing the unity and strength of the
country. The water of the Reflecting Pool cascades into the Rainbow
Pool, creating a waterfall on the western side of the plaza. Under-
neath the waterfall is an auditorium.

In conceiving his plan, St.Florian intently studied the McMillan plan of
1901 and recognized that his design needed to draw on the iconic power of
the Washington Monument to the east and the Lincoln Memorial to the west.
Thus, St.Florian intended to reinforce the east-west vista of the McMillan
Plan by using the berms as a framing device.[45]

In explaining the selection of the St.Florian design, the chair of the design
jury, David M. Childs,[46] observed that the site demanded both simplicity and
a landscape solution. He noted that he found some of the entrant concepts
"beautiful and meaningful" and having "enormous force and power," but they
were not appropriate to the location. "So we picked out of those submissions
the one we thought could be adopted and done in a landscape solution that
would be powerful enough to symbolize the importance of the event that was
being memorialized and sit properly within the setting." Hugh Hardy, who
served on both the jury and the evaluation board agreed, stating, "The big
gestures were so clear and evocative, they won the day."[47]

The process that Bill Lacy designed succeeded not only in yielding an outcome, but also invested a group of highly influential individuals in a project of
national importance. Having the allegiance of a peer group of such noted per-
sonalities would certainly assist in the next phase of the program.

Upon returning to New York, Childs wrote to Williams to commend him
in his role of facilitating the design jury: "You did a masterful job at our Blair
House Meeting. My many thanks and congratulations."[48]

With both selection groups arriving at the same decision midweek, Williams invited his fellow SDC colleagues to come to Washington that Friday to

show off the winning design. The next morning, St.Florian, while getting his hair clipped in a Providence barber shop, got the message to call Bill Lacy. Told of the results of the recent proceedings, the Rhode Islander was informed that the final decision remained weeks away.

On November 6, the SDC met to affirm the decisions reached by the two judging panels and Williams turned the floor over to Bill Lacy, who briefed the small group on the pros and cons of all of the entry submissions. In addition to Helen Fagin, Melissa A. Durbin and Miguel Encinias sat in on the presentations on behalf of the Memorial Advisory Board. After a detailed discussion, the committee voted to affirm the St.Florian selection.[49]

The Memorial Advisory Board voted to accept the selection at its November 18 meeting and two days later, the ABMC followed suit. All that was needed now was the official unveiling.

Chapter Four

THE JOY OF VICTORY AND THE AGONY OF . . .

1997

ON JANUARY 17, three days before the second inauguration of the 42nd president of the United States, a large gathering of leaders from veterans' groups, members of Congress, commissioners and staff from the ABMC, members of the MAB, media, and other interested parties filed into the East Room of the White House for what proved to be more than an unveiling ceremony.

For an immigrant from Austria, the day promised to truly place Friedrich St.Florian in a national spotlight. Born in Graz in 1932 as Friedrich Florian Gartler, the future architect grew up in a small Alpine village. Though Austria had been absorbed into the Third Reich through annexation in 1938, for Friedrich, thanks to the remoteness of his village, war only became a reality with the arrival of an American soldier at his classroom, who instructed the teacher to send the children home because American forces were moving through liberating the area. Three-quarters of a century later, the architect vividly remembers the big grin and flashing white teeth of the G.I. when he walked into the room and saw the children, mostly girls, looking up at him. The twelve-year-old boy giddily went home to his mother to exclaim that school was over. Friedrich's mother hugged him. Shedding tears, she corrected him, "No, Friedrich, the war is over."[1]

Eventually earning a degree in architecture from the Technische Universität in Graz, Friedrich decided to rebrand himself to honor family members and an Italian futurist by the name of Antonio Sant'Elia, who was killed during World War I. Though some of his early modernist designs had earned him acclaim, St.Florian chose not to sit on his laurels but instead accepted a Fulbright fellowship to travel to America, where he enrolled at Columbia University. Obtaining his master's degree, St.Florian was offered an assistant professor position at the Rhode Island School of Design. The Providence-based school then sent him to teach and study at its small facility in Rome. In Rome, besides meeting his future wife, the young architect immersed himself in classical design. Over the next few decades, St.Florian won accolades for several theoretical designs and some creative proposals, and served in several positions leading to being named a dean. During his climb up the academic ladder he took advantage of teaching opportunities at the Architectural Association School of Architecture in London, the University of Texas, McGill University, the University of Utah, Massachusetts Institute of Technology, and back to Columbia University. Liberating himself from the academic grind in the early 1990s, St.Florian once again started competing for commissions. With his most recent success being selected as the design architect for the shopping and entertaining center Providence Place and a pedestrian skybridge for the Rhode Island state capital, his sudden prominence at a ceremony at the home of the president of the United States was something he found challenging to come to grips with.[2]

St.Florian stood in the East Room because, in addition to submitting the best design, he had put together a most impressive team to execute the project. Upon receiving notification that he had been selected as one of the six finalists, St.Florian was astonished to receive a check of $75,000 to complete more detailed concept drawings. However, once St.Florian read the specifications for those drawings, and the requirement to recruit talented individuals to see the project through, he understood the reasoning behind the seemingly large amount of money. St.Florian first needed to enlarge the staff of his boutique firm from two to ten. As he interviewed potential employees, the architect began his search for an "architect of record"—a firm that would assume responsibility for construction and general contracting. In one case, he was sought out. Approached by the company that had built the Korean War Veterans Memorial, St.Florian came away unimpressed. In contrast, St.Florian had a very productive discussion with George E. Hartman, a partner at the D.C.-based Hartman-Cox firm. Established in 1965, Hartman-Cox had a reputation as the "go-to" firm in the nation's capital to perform restoration work on memorials or other older structures. Hartman recommended to St.Florian that he also needed to reach out to Ray Kaskey to be the sculptor, and Jim van Sweden of the firm Oehme–van Sweden to handle the landscaping.

For sculptor work St.Florian had been familiar with the well-known Vietnam Veterans Memorial sculptor Frederick Hart, but deferred to Kaskey, who had his own impressive portfolio and a less intense personality, much to St.Florian's liking. The Pittsburgh native had studied architecture at Carnegie Mellon and Yale before becoming a sculptor. Best known for *Portlandia*, a nearly thirty-five-foot-high copper statue assembled in Portland, Oregon, a decade earlier, Kaskey had recently worked with Davis Buckley on the National Law Enforcement Memorial. A graduate of the University of Michigan, van Sweden conducted his postgraduate education in the Netherlands. In 1977, he partnered with horticulturist and landscape architect Wolfgang Oehme to found the firm of Oehme–van Sweden and Associates. Through the next two decades the D.C.-based firm won contracts within the nation's capital as well as in locations such as New York, and they revolutionized the field with a landscape design called the New American Garden Style. Both Kaskey and Oehme–van Sweden were included in the St.Florian submission. Hartman-Cox would not be included, though the firm would later be contracted to perform work on the project. Instead, St.Florian heeded a recommendation of one of his former students who now worked at Leo A. Daly, a major architectural firm founded in 1915 by Leo A. Daly Sr. and now led by his grandson Leo A. Daly III. A noted recent accomplishment of the firm was the new terminal at the Washington National Airport. Realizing the scale of this project, St.Florian decided it would be prudent to go big. Ironically, Haydn Williams had asked him, after he won the design contest, if he could make the memorial larger![3]

However, St.Florian and his winning team would have to share the spotlight that day in the White House. To Rolly Kidder's surprise, President Clinton entered the East Room with the man he had recently defeated in the November election—Senator Bob Dole. For the soon-to-be two-term president, the unveiling ceremony of a memorial that would celebrate a story of national unity provided an ideal backdrop to conduct a magnanimous gesture recognizing the lifetime achievements of one of those wounded veterans of World War II.

In awarding the nation's highest civilian honor, the Medal of Freedom, to his former opponent, the president hoped to forge a civility in the political discourse. Gracious in acceptance of the award, the Kansan poked humor at the occasion, stating that he had expected to be in the White House that January "but under slightly different circumstances."[4]

Then, in the presence of Clinton, Dole, and the large gathering, the rendering of St.Florian's winning concept was unveiled. Having previewed the design, Clinton was effusive in his praise. "I have reviewed it and it is very impressive." He added, "Fittingly, it will be flanked by the Washington Monument and the Lincoln Memorial. For if the Revolutionary War marks the birth of our republic and the Civil War its greatest trial, then surely America's triumph in World War II will forever signal the coming of our age."[5]

As next day's headlines in the *Washington Post* and the *New York Times* gushed about the president's homage to his recent opponent, Ben Forgey's critique of the design seemed nonjudgmental, noting that the plaza created between the two sets of columns reminded him of Gian Lorenzo Bernini's piazza at St. Peter's Cathedral in Rome. However, in his discussion of the St. Florian design, Robert Gee of the *Baltimore Sun* was a bit more circumspect. He captured positive sentiments about the proposed layout from ABMC spokesman Joe Purka and John Parsons of the NPS, who observed, "There was a general fear that we were going to build a triumphal arch obstructing the east-west vista." However, Gee also damped the rah-rah of the unveiling by noting negative correspondence about the site selection that had appeared in the *Washington Post*, and a letter of concern from Senator Robert Kerrey to Secretary of the Interior Bruce Babbitt on the importance of preserving the vista. In a matter-of-fact observation, Gee quoted one of the attendees as saying, "If no one thinks it's suitable then we go back to the drawing board." That the individual quoted was CFA secretary Charles Atherton should have been a red flag.[6]

At the ceremony, Kidder also observed individuals studying the renderings with a critical eye. Standing beside his fellow New Yorker and longtime political acquaintance Senator Daniel Patrick Moynihan, Kidder noted, "He seemed rather cool about it." Afterward, Williams confided to Kidder that Moynihan, a friend from his graduate school days at Fletcher, had approached him with concerns about the design and the location.[7]

In his *Baltimore Sun* piece, Gee also mentioned the "staggering" budget projected at $100 million, in contrast to the Korean War Veterans Memorial, which cost $16 million, and the Vietnam War Veterans Memorial, which came in at half that. In retrospect, Kidder would later observe that the hiccup in the design competition that added months to the timeline was probably a blessing in disguise, since it allowed Major General Herrling to increase the staff at ABMC and bring on needed consultants. With the need for larger spaces to support the growing staff, ABMC would leave the Pulaski Building for a newer building across the Potomac River in Arlington. In some good news on the fundraising side, a consultant reported that a response rate on initial direct-mail appeals of 2.37 percent was well over the standard response rate, and the selling point of having a loved one placed on a "Registry of Remembrance" resonated with families of those who served overseas and on the home front.[8]

Despite that positive report in the aftermath of the celebratory unveiling at the White House, Williams thought out loud on paper about that daunting fundraising task, and about how little headway had been made in getting a commitment for support on Capitol Hill. Writing about the agreement memorandum reached between the ABMC and the MAB on February 8 of the previous year, Williams underlined that "it's simply not working." Outlining the organizational responsibilities and periodic meeting schedules, he concluded that a bloated infrastructure could undermine the fundraising effort. With regards to the memorial's design, which had been determined in a national competition, the MAB's involvement—excepting Helen Fagin—was no longer necessary.[9]

Williams' thinking was reflected in a letter ABMC chairman Gen. Fred Woerner wrote to MAB chair Peter Wheeler on February 28, 1997. Acknowledging the contributions Fagin was making to the Site and Design Committee and other efforts of the presidentially appointed board, the general drove home the central concern: "Pete, I ask that you and your board members commit your best efforts to the fundraising challenge."[10]

In the interim, Williams forged ahead with his monthly SDC meetings with the knowledge that the St.Florian design would never become reality without the approval of the bodies that finally had come into agreement on the site. On the horizon lay a July 24 appearance before the Commission of Fine Arts, followed a week later by a presentation to the National Capital Planning Commission. As the person who interfaced with the MAB on Williams' committee, Helen Fagin reported back to her colleagues about concerns on the design that were being addressed.

Reflecting the concerns of Senator Moynihan and others, at the February 10 SDC meeting, Williams challenged St.Florian to review the mass of the berms, the size of the rebuilt Rainbow Pool, and the height of the columns, and to make sure that everything complied with the Americans with Disabilities Act. To give St.Florian room to scale down his design, the ABMC removed the requirement for an indoor auditorium. Days earlier in the *Washington Post*,

Williams had stated, "Our thinking has been changed, and we are scaling down the amount of enclosed spaced considerably."[11]

Four weeks later, St.Florian and members of his design team returned to Washington with scaled-down drawings showing reduced forty-foot high columns and the berm rising to fifty feet in elevation over the surroundings. The level of the Rainbow Pool would drop to twelve feet below street level. Williams and his team had anxiously awaited the revised drawings because, during the intervening period, Senator Robert Kerrey had issued a February 20 press release vocalizing his opposition to the proposed design at the Rainbow Pool site. Speaking to a reporter with the *New York Times* following his public announcement of opposition, Kerrey observed, "This is a permanent haircut. Once it is done, this will not grow back."[12]

Kerrey's opposition was drawing the attention of his colleagues. Following his return in early April from the western Pacific, having attended the twenty-first anniversary of the signing of the Covenant of the Northern Marianas that he had negotiated, Williams responded to an inquiry from Senator Daniel Inouye, arguing that the scaled-down version of the winning St.Florian design would preserve the broad central vista that Kerrey argued for maintaining in his press release. As further reassurance, Williams reminded the heroic Hawaiian World War II veteran that the CFA and the NCPC "would continue to serve as guardians for aesthetic, symbolic purposes." To further make the case that the memorial would enhance the Mall, Williams invited Inouye to tour the site or arrange to have Major General Herrling brief him.[13]

Fortunately for Williams in his future dealings with Capitol Hill, the ABMC had just recruited a powerful ally. At the White House Medal of Freedom ceremony that had been paired with the World War II Memorial unveiling, Senator Dole felt doubly honored, since the occasion allowed him "to honor some others who are more entitled." With those evocative words, it became readily apparent who could fill the void for a National World War II Memorial Campaign. Major General Herrling visited Dole on two occasions to reel the Kansan in. Herrling recalled that Dole had been hesitant. "He had been burned" previously, having lent his name to be associated with the Battle of Normandy Foundation. The nonprofit organization, formed in 1985, had squandered much of the $14.7 million it had raised, including some $3 million from a U.S. Treasury coin sale. On his second visit, Herrling assured Dole that he would be continuously briefed on the status of memorial finances and that a campaign cochair from the corporate sector would be brought in to serve. On March 19, 1997, Senator Dole accepted the ABMC offer to take on this critical role.[14]

Unfortunately, concerns were not only being expressed on Capitol Hill but also in the media, with pundits taking shots at the design in such journals and newspapers as *Time*, the *Boston Globe*, the *Chicago Tribune*, the *New York Times*, and the *Washington Times*. Of particular concern, Deborah Dietsch in *Architecture* savaged St. Florian's design as "painfully reminiscent of the designs by Nazi architect Albert Speer." Though he understood that Washington's other monuments had all generated negative reviews, Williams sought some reassurance and guidance on the course they had chosen through convening two gatherings in mid-April. First, the Rhode Island School of Design hosted a symposium to discuss the World War II Memorial design competition and the elements that led to the St. Florian design. Following that conclave, Williams and St. Florian traveled to Manhattan to meet with alumni of the Architect-Engineer Evaluation Board and the design jury to receive constructive criticisms of the reworked design.[15]

Recommendations were also coming from other sources. MAB member Miguel Encinias had faulted the St. Florian design for a lack of symbolism. In response, MAB member Jon A. Mangis suggested to Helen Fagin that the SDC should consider incorporating the Gold Star into the design, noting the symbolism of the Gold Star lapel pin worn by Gold Star mothers and members of the American War Orphans network. Fagin wrote back to the director of Veterans Affairs in Oregon that the idea was worthy of consideration, noting that the war had claimed the lives of more than 400,000 Americans.[16]

After more than a week to digest and contemplate the comments received at the Rhode Island and New York gatherings as well as absorb other input, Williams again convened the SDC in the nation's capital on May 1 to discuss what recommendations should be incorporated or ignored. With consensus reached on recommended changes calling for a grander west side entrance and improving the ceremonial entrance on 17th Street, St.Florian had his marching orders to return in less than two weeks with revised drawings for another SDC meeting, on the eve of one of the semi-annual ABMC commissioner meetings.[17]

On May 13, 1997, General Woerner convened the 123rd meeting of the ABMC. Regarding the World War II Memorial, the commission had an opportunity to preview the latest design changes, and to hear an overview from Williams on the ongoing design process and forthcoming approval steps before the CFA and NCPC at the end of July. In further positive news, the White House unveiling of a design had generated a solid response to a test mailing of 86,372 pieces sent out immediately after the event, generating an average give of $33.30. Based on that success, another 1,444,984 letters with General Woerner's signature were sent out in early April. A follow-on mailing of more than 2.6 million letters was set for June. Perhaps the best news overall was that Senator Dole's signature on that letter symbolized the campaign had a leader. However, that leader had agreed to take the mantel with the caveat that he would soon share it with a cochair, who would be identified from the private sector.[18]

Despite the unanticipated opposition in Congress and in the architectural community, Williams felt confident that the St.Florian design would win the day at the forthcoming CFA hearing and with good reason. J. Carter Brown had blind copied him on a letter he had written to two of Senator Joseph Lieberman's constituents in response to concerns they raised about St.Florian's design following the publication of the Dietsch editorial. In response to Dietsch's criticism, Brown lavished praise on the design, which was "reminiscent of Bernini's solution for the forecourt of St. Peter's," and recounted the recent symposium held in Rhode Island with the six finalists discussing their proposals. "I was there all day, and was persuaded, as was the architectural critic of the *Washington Post*, and, I felt, the entire audience, that the St.Florian design was clearly the winner."[19]

Armed with such inside knowledge, Williams convened only one more meeting of the SDC during the buildup period, to make a few additional tweaks to address some of the criticisms. At the June 30 session, St.Florian produced some new designs that raised the level of the Rainbow Pool to just seven and a half feet below grade and further reduced the size of the berms, columns, and interior spaces. However, Senator Kerrey remained adamant in his opposition even to the scaled-down design. A crushing editorial in the July 4 edition of the *New York Times*, "Hallowed Ground is in Jeopardy: Keep the Mall As It Is," served as a further warning of the battle ahead and a call to general quarters.[20]

As Helen Fagin prepared a rebuttal to the *New York Times* editorial, arguing that "the site and design are fully compatible with the objectives of a great national monument on the nation's mall," Peter Wheeler sent a memorandum to members of the MAB warning of an organizing opposition and that Major General Herrling had initiated a plan of action to reach out to members of Congress, veterans' groups, and other parties to demonstrate support for the St.Florian design. Wheeler urged his board to contact their representatives and ask them to sign a letter of support. By mid-July, that letter had attained ninety-eight signatures. Separately, Williams approached members of the Architect-Engineer Evaluation Board and the design jury to come to Washington for the CFA hearing.[21]

As Herrling, Wheeler, and Williams rallied the troops, St.Florian suddenly had some time on his hands. The ABMC offered him an opportunity to return to his native continent to tour several of the ABMC monuments and cemeteries. The indoctrination trip would prove to be a worthwhile investment. In addition to visiting the American World War II cemeteries in the Netherlands, Belgium, Luxembourg, France, and England, St.Florian viewed some of the World War I cemeteries. St.Florian's British driver also insisted he take a look at nearby British war dead burial grounds for comparison. Between the American World War I and II cemeteries, St.Florian observed that, thanks to General Pershing and Paul Cret, the architecture on the World War I memorial structures seemed superior, while the siting for the World War II cemeteries, as typified by the American Normandy Cemetery, was more dramatic. As for the British grounds, St.Florian came away impressed that the British allowed for small inscriptions submitted by family to be placed on the grave markers. Coming upon one marker, the architect paused to read, "To the world he was a soldier—to us he was the world."[22]

On July 24, J. Carter Brown convened the Commission of Fine Arts to evaluate the ABMC design proposal for the Rainbow Pool site. Ambassador Williams provided a lengthy and passionate statement on the objectives that the ABMC had sought in the winning design. He then turned the floor over to St.Florian, who espoused an urban design strategy that aimed to use the berms as a means to "orchestrate" the unobstructed view from the stairs of the Lincoln Memorial eastward to the Washington Monument. His placement of a waterfall between the ground level of the Lincoln Memorial Reflecting Pool and the now depressed Rainbow Pool aimed to optically connect the two water features. The fifty columns represented the forty-eight states as well as the two major territories that had suffered from significant enemy action—Hawaii and Alaska. St.Florian also delved into a unique aspect of his column design that cut off their caps. In the Roman and Greek traditions, the symbolism represented those slain with their promising years still ahead. Congresswoman Marcy Kaptur, the author of the enabling legislation, asked, "What could be more appropriate, as we stand at the crossroads of the twentieth and twenty-first centuries, than to dedicate a memorial on the Mall to our nation's finest hour of the twentieth century?" In her remarks, Kaptur noted that she now had the support of 160 of her house colleagues, as well as that of ten senators.

An impressive list of individuals turned out on behalf of the Williams, St.Florian, and Kaptur presentations thanks to the mobilization efforts of

ABMC and MAB leadership. The man who had served as the guiding hand for the design competition, Bill Lacy, stated, "The simplicity, the directness, the clarity of this design is appropriate." However, what caught the media's attention were the number of individuals who chose to spend a Thursday in the middle of summer to voice their opposition to the modified plan of what had been unveiled six months earlier. Leading the charge was Senator Kerrey, who had recruited nineteen of his fellow senators to sign a letter to Secretary of the Interior Bruce Babbitt to protest the site selection and design approval process. Much to Rolly Kidder's disappointment, the list included his good acquaintance, Senator Moynihan. In the wake of that letter, both Kerrey and Lacy appeared with Jim Lehrer on the PBS show *Newshour* to debate the proposed memorial. Echoing what he had stated before J. Carter Brown's panel on national television, Kerrey expressed concern of the memorial's construction on a flood plain, its interference with the contemplative simplicity of the Mall, and that an environmental assessment had yet to be completed. "This is a significantly large memorial that will change the nature of the Mall," argued the Nebraskan senator, further stating, "I believe it is too large, I believe it is too intrusive, I believe this is too hallowed a ground to build anything more on it." Picking up on the hallowed ground argument—many civil rights activists had stood at the location to hear Martin Luther King Jr.'s "I have a dream" speech delivered nearly thirty-four years earlier—the District of Columbia's delegate to Congress, Eleanor Holmes Norton, declared that the site should be "permanently declared off limits to monuments." In contrast to Kerrey and Holmes Norton, Judith Scott Feldman, a professor of art and architectural history at American University, took issue with St. Florian's design as giving the space the feel of a recreational area. She urged a complete redesign to incorporate contemplative features.[23]

After hours of passionate arguments for the two competing viewpoints, the CFA voted. Secretary Charles Atherton summed it up, "The design didn't fly." However, the commission remained unanimous in its approval of the Rainbow Pool site, a blow to many of the opponents who sought to move the memorial elsewhere. J. Carter Brown explained, "We will never find a subject more fitting for this site." In explaining their rejection of the St.Florian design, the commission found the design too large and elaborate. Brown would echo Ben Forgey's earlier critique that the requirement for interior exhibition spaces amounted to the construction of a museum on the Mall and that it was an ill-advised objective. There was consensus that the berms were, indeed, intrusive and that the removal of the elm trees was uncalled for.

A week later both sides presented similar testimony before Harvey Gantt and the National Capital Planning Commission, with a similar outcome. In contrast to the unanimous CFA vote to keep the site, the NCPC chose to retain the site with a 7–4 majority.

Between the two scheduled hearings, Rolly Kidder had finally convinced Haydn Williams to relax a bit and join him to spend time some time at his lakefront residence in western New York. Following the July 24 vote of the CFA, the two men set off on a long quiet drive out away from the nation's capital.

Chapter Five

THE COMEBACK

1997–98

O N AUGUST 12, 1997, the *Baltimore Sun* reported on the unex-
pected double rejection of the St.Florian design: "Within the next
few weeks, the American Battle Monuments Commission, sponsor
of the World War II project, will meet to decide how to regroup in time to
make another presentation to the two agencies this fall. According to commission spokesman Joe Purka, the panel will choose between reworking the current plan or returning to the drawing board for a new design. 'Right now, that's
completely undecided,' he said."[1]

The seven-hour drive from Washington, D.C., to the new Kidder home-
stead on Lake Chautauqua near Jamestown, New York, was a somber one.
Haydn Williams reflected on the swirl of controversy that had besieged and
threatened to upend this honorable tribute, which the nation had promised
to those who had served during the greatest global conflict in human history.
Rolly Kidder recalled, "Haydn wasn't just sad—he was angry. He felt that
the floor had been pulled out from under us by the CFA." As Kidder navi-
gated northward through the state highways of western Pennsylvania, the

two men discussed the options. Williams understood that another national competition would add at least another year to the project. The youngest of the World War II veterans were now in their seventies, a fact reflected by Congresswoman Kaptur speaking to reporters after the design turndown: "We are losing our World War II veterans, so there is an urgency to these proceedings."

Arriving at the lakefront property, Williams retired to the guestroom to get a good night's sleep. The next morning, the ambassador enjoyed a hardy breakfast courtesy of Rolly's wife Jane. As the three finished their morning meal, Williams turned to his hosts to ask if he could use the house phone: "I need to call Friedrich." In Rhode Island, Friedrich picked up the ringing phone and heard a familiar voice: "How are you doing, Friedrich?" Understandably, the architect was not in the best of spirits. Williams tried to be conciliatory, noting that the CFA's feedback still applauded the concept of lowering the Rainbow Pool. Indeed, on July 30, J. Carter Brown had written to General Woerner to also commend the design for its maintenance of the open vista and for its water features.[2] Then a thought struck Williams midway through a sentence: "Have you ever heard of Gen. Oliver P. Smith?" From the silence coming from the other end of the phone call, Kidder correctly guessed that St.Florian was dumbfounded. Kidder recalled Williams explaining, "Well, Friedrich, he was a Marine general during the Korean War at the time the Chinese entered the war. His outfit was surrounded by about 300,000 Chinese troops at a place called the Chosin Reservoir and it was the middle of winter. The Marines were in a tight, untenable spot and had to pull out. And, do you know what Smith said when asked by a member of the press as to whether he was retreating? He said, 'Retreat, hell! We're not retreating, we're just advancing in a different direction!'"[3]

Williams then asked, "Friedrich, are you willing to continue to be our designer but move in a different direction to get the World War II Memorial built?" It did not take long for St.Florian to ponder and come back with a response. Yes, he would like to continue to work on designing the memorial.

Previously, in an interview in the *New York Times*, St.Florian had admitted that he had been taken aback by the controversy: "Quite frankly, I did not expect it. The initial response nationwide was very positive, extremely laudatory." He had not been offended by the CFA's questioning of the need for interior exhibition space. St.Florian later credited Benjamin Forgey of the *Washington Post* with the sentiment that "a memorial is not a school—it is a shrine. A memorial is not to teach—it is to inspire."[4] Freedom from the exhibition space requirement opened numerous creative options for St.Florian to pursue with the SDC.

Concluding his chat, Williams hung up the phone. Kidder could see the relief in his face. "He then smiled and looked out at the lake," Kidder recalled decades later. "This has been a bump in the road," he said. "But now, with Friedrich's help and a lot of work from all of us, there is a way forward." With that, Kidder took his guest to a local pub for lunch and to meet friends. A refreshed and reinvigorated Williams flew back to Washington from Buffalo the next day to meet with Major General Herrling and the staff. Following the NCPC meeting, Williams caught a flight home to San Francisco.

Independently, Helen Fagin had reached a similar conclusion. In a memorandum to Herrling and Williams, she wrote, "I came to the realization that we must reexamine our original approach to the memorial's design program. Regretfully, the functional and educational elements of our design have been rejected and seem to be outright unacceptable by both commissions. Indeed, both commissions strongly recommended a strictly symbolic memorial, surrounded by water and appropriate landscaping."[5]

The design was not the only element of the project to undergo scrutiny. Months earlier, the ABMC had signed a contract with the New York–based public relations firm of Burson-Marsteller for an annual fee of $1,067,000. In the wake of the July 4, 1997, *New York Times* editorial and other harsh critiques in the media, the ABMC's public affairs point man, Joe Purka, drafted a point paper summarizing the PR support arrangement, noting "positive publicity can never be guaranteed." Somewhat skeptical, Williams penned a note on the paper suggesting that an ad hoc committee be formed at the next ABMC commissioners meeting, to review the depth of the relationship with the PR firm. To Burson-Marsteller's credit, the New York firm grasped the gravity of the design rejection and how it could drain strong public support. The firm adjusted its messaging with a new series of public service announcements, using images of World War II veterans with the words, "What you did changed the world—don't let it fade away."[6]

The design upheaval also led to some internal introspection on fundraising. Fortunately, the June mailout of more than 2 million appeals before the berm concept rejection was yielding a solid return, with an average contribution of thirty-five dollars. However, with no promises for federal construction monies forthcoming, ABMC and its campaign chair, Senator Dole, hoped the difference could be made up in the corporate sector. Understanding that business connections had limits, Dole wisely recruited Frederick W. Smith, the CEO of Federal Express, to serve as his campaign cochair. With the announcement of Smith as cochairman on August 19, 1997, the campaign had brought on board a Marine veteran of the Vietnam War who had a personal motivation to honor his father and three uncles, all of whom had served during the earlier global conflict.[7]

As the CEO of an extremely successful corporation that daily interacted with not only hundreds of domestic businesses but also overseas corporations, Smith had amassed a huge Rolodex of corporate counterparts. In the first few months, Smith had helped land nearly $5 million in domestic corporate donations. Past ABMC policy had been ambivalent about accepting contributions from overseas corporations. In the case of the World War II Memorial, there was consensus that donations from German and Japanese corporations would be awkward, but Fred Smith saw no heartburn in going after corporations headquartered in World War II allied nations. However, others within the ABMC disagreed. Williams sided with Smith. Seeing the policy paper recommending that no foreign donations be accepted, the former ambassador wrote that "an embarrassment hardly bespeaks a great nation, a grateful nation." In contrast, while contributions from nations such as the United Kingdom, Canada, and France were frowned on, the ABMC had no issues accepting funds from "ATF" (alcohol, tobacco & firearms) companies such as Anheuser-Busch, Philip Morris, or Remington Arms, because these corporations had made significant contributions to the war effort in the 1940s.[8]

When Williams reconvened the SDC on September 9, the small group reviewed the feedback provided by the two commissions as a starting point for concept papers that they would swap over the next few weeks. All concurred with maintaining St. Florian's sunken plaza concept. Rolly Kidder hoped to retain the colonnade element symbolizing "unity of nation embraced around a common purpose." Kidder also proposed one side of the pool be "dedicated to our dead and missing from the war." In addition, the Navy Vietnam War veteran offered options on how to treat the approach to the Rainbow Pool from 17th Street, to include either a chronological walk through the war tracking the mounting casualty rate, a path flanked by historical quotations, or a stroll through representations of American overseas cemeteries.[9]

Based on the feedback from J. Carter Brown, Helen Fagin contended that salvaging the colonnade was a lost cause unless the columns were redesigned. She noted that, with no interior spaces, any story needed to be told in words or artistic elements. As for the approach from 17th Street, Fagin wrote, "To make the cemeteries the focal point of the memorial walk, would, I believe, make it too morbid. Rather, we would want to elevate the spirit of the visitor with an uplifting message the American experience in World War II has to offer both on the home front and in our global engagement." Here Fagin struck a chord with Williams, who underlined this passage on his copy.[10]

Besides serving as a launching point for new creative concepts, the September 9 meeting produced a realization that the scope of the content that the new memorial should communicate was beyond the comprehension of those sitting around the table. Thought was given to form a content subcommittee, to include veterans, historians, and writers—sort of an honorary advisory board—to help discern the more significant World War II story lines that needed conveyance.

In the wake of the September 9 meeting, thought also was given to how to redesign the memorial to surmount objections and placate one of the memorial's fiercest critics, Senator Bob Kerrey. Writing to Kerrey on September 18, 1997, Williams reviewed with the senator the "musts" for the memorial. The design needed to be "commensurate" with the significance of the conflict, possess "memorable landmark qualities," and feature "great architectural and aesthetic merit." Finally, Williams understood that Kerrey desired that the design be respectful of the surroundings.

By involving Kerrey in the redesign discussions, Williams hoped to convert an adamant opponent into a staunch champion. Kerrey appreciated an opportunity to compromise on the design, given that his stand had not won him friendships with Roger Durbin and hundreds of thousands of other survivors from the Greatest Generation. Those survivors and their friends and families were making their support for the memorial known through their checkbooks. As summer turned to fall, the campaign treasurer noted the campaign had already grossed nearly $43 million. However, nearly $27 million of that had been eaten up by the expenses associated with the design competition and initiating fundraising and marketing campaigns.[11]

Up in Providence, St.Florian and his team worked on a redesign. A St.Florian creative element that began to take shape during this time frame: facing identical arches anchoring the north and south ends of the Rainbow Pool, each representing the two major theaters of the war—the Atlantic and the Pacific. Back in Washington, Williams brought the SDC together for an early December gathering to review St.Florian's architectural progress. While the Austrian immigrant had a brilliant capacity to form shapes into structures, Williams felt it incumbent on the SDC to provide the intellectual grounding to make those structures meaningful. The content subcommittee idea was revisited. Subsequently, five days after the final SDC for 1997, Helen Fagin received a letter from General Woerner:

Dear Helen:

Ambassador Haydn Williams, in his capacity as Chairman of the World War II Memorial Site and Design Committee, has recommended there be constituted a subordinate panel to address the challenge of the Memorial's content. I enthusiastically endorse his recommendation and am delighted that you consented to chair this panel.[12]

Drawing from her experience with the United States Holocaust Museum, Fagin impressed upon the committee that collecting content and organizing that content to tell a story required two different skill sets. Fagin happened to have someone in mind and reached out to Ralph Appelbaum who headed Ralph Appelbaum Associates (RAA), one of the world's largest museum exhibition design firms. Having served on the Holocaust Museum's Content and Education committees, Fagin had developed a good working relationship with Appelbaum, who had counted the Washington museum among his clients, and she suggested that his firm submit a proposal.

Appelbaum did just that on December 19. Reading his copy of the document that had arrived at his San Francisco condominium via facsimile before Christmas, Williams underlined Appelbaum's intent to discuss "our role in developing the visitor experience, message, and function of the World War II Memorial." He noted the proposed four-month consultation window and fee. What caught Williams' attention (and where he drew a second underline) was the passage: "RAA shall have copyright on resulting work until such time as the plan is implemented, built, installed, and completed by RAA."[13]

Though turned off by the presumption of this last proposed term, Williams urged Major General Herrling to pursue an arrangement. On January 15, 1998, Ralph Appelbaum made the initial outreach to visit Friedrich St.Florian at his Providence studio to get acquainted. However, a week later Williams got a call from Herrling. Apparently, St.Florian had already contracted with Edwin Schlossberg, another museum exhibition consultant who had been working with him for a year. Schlossberg, well known on the Washington social scene as the husband of Caroline Kennedy, expressed dismay that ABMC had reached out to a competing firm and demanded an explanation and an apology. This placed Williams in an awkward situation. Once again thinking out loud onto his legal pad, Williams weighed his options. After talking to St.Florian, who preferred to retain Schlossberg, the former ambassador sought a diplomatic way to make amends. Ralph Appelbaum withdrew his consultation offer.[14]

To provide Schlossberg with content guidance, Fagin fleshed out her SDC subcommittee. Rather than reaching out to veterans, historians, and writers, Fagin populated her new little group with MAB members and ABMC commissioners, to include Rear Admiral Chang, Brigadier General Foote, and Brigadier General Kinnard, as well as Commissioner Kidder. Ambassador Williams served in an ex officio capacity. This group gathered on February 23 for a St.Florian "Work in Progress" presentation. The architect would not disappoint. In the aftermath of the design competition, Williams had enlisted several members of the Architect-Engineer Evaluation Board and the design jury to volunteer to serve on a sounding-board panel, to include Max Bond, Robert Campbell, David Childs, Ed Feiner, Hugh Hardy, Ada Louise Huxtable, Bill Lacy, and Laurie Olin. St.Florian met with this group on several occasions in New York and Washington in the months following the July rejections, and the influences of these talented individuals would make their way onto paper.[15]

Eyes squinted and heads nodded with approval as the Rhode Islander unveiled his drawings. With no need to construct berms and by shrinking the size of the Rainbow Pool by 15 percent, St.Florian spared the need for chainsaws, preserving the rows of elm trees that were an element of the McMillan plan. Fagin especially liked St.Florian's treatment of the approach from 17th Street with parallel ramps/staircases. Those walking toward the memorial on those flanking pavements from 17th Street would observe that St.Florian retained the waterfalls feature of his first design, which provided the illusion of water flowing from the Reflecting Pool into a now oval-shaped plaza. The new design featured two waterfalls on the west side of the plaza, bracketing the sacred precinct that Kidder had envisioned in earlier discussions. The sub-committee bandied about the concept of installing a Torch of Freedom within this area.

St.Florian's new drawings addressed several practical matters. To the south of the memorial, St.Florian proposed a cutoff from 17th Street to handle tour buses and handicap parking. To the north, he recommended a tour-mobile stop on Constitution Avenue. As the meeting came to a close, an air of opti-mism permeated the room. The ABMC had arranged for the new designs to be considered at an upcoming May 21 hearing of the CFA and a following June 4 meeting of the NCPC.[16]

Taking pride in the new design like the father of a newborn child, Wil-liams carried the revised St.Florian portfolio around the nation's capital to show off his new baby and prepare the battlespace for the upcoming reviews of the two commissions. While having breakfast with John Parsons at the Cosmos Club on March 3, Williams learned that upper echelons within the Department of the Interior were pleased with the new drawings. Parsons pre-dicted that Williams should not expect difficulty with obtaining NCPC approval, but advised that in making their presentation, Williams need not push forward a long line of veterans to make testimonials. The ambassador acknowledged the advice but reiterated that, for political purposes, they still would want to have one or two vets speak on behalf of the new design. Parsons shrugged in an understanding way. Regarding the testimony of noted Man-hattan architect David Childs, Parsons surprised Williams with his observa-tion that Childs would hold more sway with the CFA. Regarding the NCPC, Williams recorded Parsons' parochial observation: "Word around town was New York having too much influence on design."[17]

One of the surprising names on the list of senators that Kerrey had amassed to oppose the site and design of the World War II Memorial was Strom Thur-mond. The South Carolina Republican had been Congresswoman Kaptur's ally in the Senate, from when he first helped her introduce legislation autho-rizing the World War II Memorial in 1988. Upon receiving the draft of a letter being prepared for Thurmond to sign, which would be sent to the president restating his opposition to the Rainbow Pool site, Williams quickly drafted preemptive strike correspondence to the senator, which stated, "The content of the letter you were asked to sign contains many inaccuracies and misstatements of fact." Williams continued, "I therefore implore you to give us an opportunity to be heard so that you have a balanced and factual basis for your judgment."

The plea was too late. Thurmond joined with Kerrey in signing the letter, which argued that the memorial would ruin the Mall vista of two of the capital's most significant landmarks. From a public relations standpoint, the letter's coverage in the media represented a setback. However, Williams was not going to give up on Thurmond. He then arranged for Senator Dole to send his former Senate colleague a briefing paper on the latest design changes. That got Thurmond's attention. The Carolinian wrote back, appreciating the briefing paper and exclaiming, "Bob, I want to assure you I stand as an ally and not an obstacle." Dole wrote back to say that Major General Herrling would be in touch with Thurmond's chief of staff to arrange for follow-on briefings.[18]

Williams updated the ABMC at the 125th commissioners' meeting on April 7, and the MAB when they met a month later on May 5. Having convinced Senator Thurmond to be more open-minded about the project, the next step would be to convince Senator Kerrey that the new design addressed the list of "musts" that had been put forward. To do so, a new "unveil" was arranged for May 12. Stepping before a large crowd of reporters, Haydn Williams proclaimed, "When built, the World War II Memorial will indeed be a place for commemoration and commitment." He continued, "It will be a place for joyful celebration of the American spirit—a special moment in our national history which should not be forgotten, a time when America saved the world, a time which forever changed the face of American life and the direction of world history." Then St.Florian followed Williams at the podium, a situation he was getting accustomed to: "We were cognizant of the significance of the site—its parklike setting." Though not conducted at the White House, the event had its desired effect—favorable coverage in the media. In her article in the next day's

Washington Post, Linda Wheeler reported how the new design eliminated the structural elements that had led the CFA and the NCPC "to reject the original design last year."[19]

Buoyed by the positive reaction to the revamped design, Williams called on Senator Kerrey the next day to discuss the way forward. With St.Florian's new design further addressing the vista objection, the Nebraska senator relented. A week later he held a press conference to announce his support for the revised World War II Memorial design. In his remarks, he lauded Marcy Kaptur and Strom Thurmond for their introduction of the legislation, Bob Dole and Haydn Williams for their advocacy on behalf of ABMC, and finally, he commended Friedrich St.Florian for a job well done in responding to criticism. However, Kerrey was not finished. One fundraising brainstorm idea that had been discussed at the recent meeting of the MAB was to approach each state to appropriate one dollar to honor each servicemember of that state who served in the military during the war. Kerrey took pleasure in announcing that on June 2, Governor Ben Nelson of Nebraska would present Senator Dole with a check for $52,900, making Nebraska the first state to make such a donation to support the national fundraising campaign. However, perhaps the more significant contribution Kerrey made was the timing of the press conference, a day ahead of the May 21 hearing before J. Carter Brown's Commission of Fine Arts.[20]

As if not to leave anything to chance, on the morning of the hearing the national newspaper *USA Today* featured a forum coauthored by Senator Dole and Presidents Gerald Ford, Jimmy Carter, and George H. W. Bush, discussing how they had served their country, left the service to start families, and went on to further serve the nation, not forgetting that many of their contemporaries had made a far greater sacrifice. In conclusion, the four senior statesmen reminded their countrymen to remember those who had given their lives for freedom during the upcoming Memorial Day, and of the importance of having a World War II memorial as a permanent tribute to those who served.

About one hundred people packed into the hearing room at the Commission of Fine Arts to hear the case for and against the revised design, and a verdict. Senator Kerrey's and Senator Thurmond's withdrawal of objections took the wind from the sails of the opposition. Indeed, the two senators joined with seventy-four other senators and one hundred members of the House in signing letters in support of the memorial. Joining Marcy Kaptur in testifying on behalf of the new memorial design was Virginia senator John W. Warner. Adding to the political star power, big names from the architectural world added their high praise. David Childs argued that the new design had remained faithful to the original concept (which he had initially selected as the head of the design jury) but had become more "gardenesque." This was a hat tip to fellow design juror Laurie Olin, who also lauded St.Florian's "landscape solution," which she had influenced. Once again, Williams and St.Florian had an opportunity to make their case before the commission architect, arguing that the design took inspiration from the site itself. To help illustrate his case, St.Florian produced models of the proposed site to offer a three-dimensional rendering for the Brown-led commission. In addition, at the site itself, scaffolding was installed to represent elements of the design. Seven individuals spoke in opposition. Jim McGrath complained, "No amount of plastic surgery will correct the fundamental flaw of the site selection."

However, as decided by unanimous vote at an earlier hearing, the site issue had been settled. The question before Brown's panel was the suitability of the design. Speaking last, American University professor Judith Scott Feldman argued against the revised St.Florian concept. Claiming she was now speaking on behalf of the Committee of 100, an organization of distinguished citizens founded back in 1923 with an objective to safeguard the values of the L'Enfant and McMillan plans, Feldman stated that the revised design had not addressed the concerns she raised ten months earlier. She then introduced some alternative options, including the addition of an amphitheater.

After deliberations, J. Carter Brown expressed pleasure in announcing that the commission had voted to unanimously and enthusiastically endorse the concept of the redesign.[21]

The *Washington Times* quoted Williams the next day, "We knew the revised design was eminently worthy of the site and the lasting significance of the event it commemorated, and it was gratifying to have it confirmed."

Two weeks after the CFA had approved the revised design, David Childs took a moment to repeat in writing something he had expressed to Williams verbally: "I meant what I said at the hearing—you have become a hero of mine as a result of the World War II selection and approval process. It was *your* vision, diplomacy, and perseverance that won the day."[22]

A month and a half after the CFA's highly publicized approval, the NCPC had its opportunity to weigh in on the revised St.Florian design. Though not unanimous thanks to two dissenters, the NCPC approval, with some recommendations, gave the ABMC the green light to convert the concept drawings into plans that a construction company could follow to build the commemorative structure. For Williams and St.Florian, the days of standing before the two commissions were not completely behind them, since they both had an interest and a potential say in final design element proposals. For the ABMC and its Site and Design Committee, the real work lay ahead. In the coming months the St.Florian team would be challenged to draft and redraft designs. Given the emphasis on sculptural elements, Ray Kaskey's influence grew, as the local sculptor would make substantial contributions to the memorial that stands today.

On the other hand, for Bob Dole and Fred Smith, who had taken on the burden of raising the necessary funding, public awareness would provide the cornerstone of a successful capital campaign. Fortunately, three weeks after Harvey Gantt announced NCPC approval of the St.Florian redesign, a new movie appeared in theaters across the country—*Saving Private Ryan.*

Chapter Six

TOM HANKS ARRIVES ON THE SCENE

1998–99

AVING WON approval at both the CFA hearing and the NCPC hearing for the progress being made toward a final design, the ABMC and the MAB continued to raise funds, seeking small contributions through direct mail and larger donations through corporate contributions and cause-marketing campaigns. By mid-August, at the 128th ABMC meeting, the commissioners heard from the individual who had been brought in to lead the growing fundraising team, Jim Aylward, who reported that $68 million had been raised. Of note, one of the more successful fundraising initiatives (suggested by one of Aylward's growing fundraising staff, Army Vietnam veteran John "Skip" Shannon) was to seek appropriations from individual state legislatures—a dollar to honor every individual who served from that state.

Williams noted that California had yet to follow the lead of twenty-one other states such as New York, which had authorized $1.7 million. He returned home from the commissioners' meeting to write to his assemblyman, Kevin Shelly, asking him to support California Senate Bill No. 1, to provide one

dollar for every Californian who had served in the war. With additional lobbying by the San Franciscan Williams, California joined the growing list of
states that recognized it was time to say thank you.[1]

However, the campaign still lacked the "face"—the official spokesperson
to generate further grassroots contributions. Retired news anchors Walter
Cronkite and David Brinkley, who had built their reputations on World War
II reporting, declined offers to get involved due to other obligations. Seeing
the public reaction for *Saving Private Ryan*, which showcased the ABMC
Normandy American Cemetery overlooking Omaha beach, Major General
Herrling sent a letter to the Oscar-winning actor Tom Hanks on August 12,
1998, asking if he would be willing to serve as the campaign spokesperson.
Three weeks later, Herrling received a letter with an affirmative response. In a
follow-on phone call, General Woerner recalled Hanks telling him, "I'm your
man."[2]

Hanks proved to be more than true to his commitment. At the People's
Choice Awards held at the Pasadena Civic Center on January 13, 1999, Hanks
was honored with the best film actor award for his role as Capt. John H. Miller
in *Saving Private Ryan*. Stepping up to the podium before a celebratory audience, Hanks offered repeated thanks for the cheers and then broke out a prepared statement and began reading:

> Now the men that were portrayed by myself and the other cast
> members of *Saving Private Ryan* were a collection of ordinary
> Americans who did nothing less than to help save the world a half a
> century ago. Now this generation of men, who are our fathers and
> uncles and husbands and brothers, are sadly leaving us at a rate of
> about one thousand a day. If I may, let me take this venue of a nation-
> wide coast-to-coast broadcast to give you a special phone number
> that some of you might want to call. Nowhere in our nation's capital
> along the Mall will you find the memorial built for those who died
> in World War II. It has yet to be built. The site has been selected. The

design has been made a reality. Just a couple of bucks from everyone watching at home tonight and a few more from those who feel so inclined will make possible the creation of a place [where] we can honor forever the generation that defined an era and preserved our way of life. Here's the 1-800 number—it's easy to remember: 1-800-639-4WW2. Give what you can as a tribute. It's the World War II Memorial Campaign—1-800-639-4992. It won't itself change our world, but it will honor those Americans who did.

Major General Herrling recalled the overwhelmingly positive response to the Hanks call to action. That evening the campaign 1-800 line received some 19,000 calls, and another 11,000 calls flooded in on the following day. Given Hanks' initiative to promote the cause at the People's Choice Awards, General Woerner and General Herrling would task Col. Mike Conley, who succeeded Colonel Purka as director of communications, with the chore of working further with Hanks. Conley had experience working with Hollywood during his service in the Air Force, and the retired colonel recalled that Hanks was most cordial and very generous with his time. Working with the campaign's public relations and advertising firm Burson-Marsteller, Hanks agreed to do a series of public service announcements that generated additional contributions. This was contingent on convincing the Ad Council to take on the World War II Memorial cause. The Ad Council is a nonprofit organization consisting of leaders from multimedia, advertising, marketing, and public relation firms. It selects causes to support and runs campaigns for the advertising agencies that create the promotion media for newspapers, radio, television, and those respective media outlets donating the time and space to distribute the pitch. Though the origins of the Ad Council date back to the dawn of World War II with the creation of the War Advertising Council, the focus of the organization in the 1990s concentrated on youth issues. However, the ABMC indirectly had a seat at the table. Ed Ney, then chairman of Marsteller Advertising—the advertising arm of Burson-Marsteller—sat on the board of the Ad

Council and successfully presented the case for the organization to take on the World War II Memorial Campaign. With the Ad Council commitment, Burson-Marsteller developed the ad concepts and scripts and coordinated photography, studio, and recording sessions out in Santa Monica, California. An initial batch of ad placements featuring Hanks was timed to appear in newspapers around the Academy Awards program, demonstrating the potential of the campaign.[3]

Mike Conley recalled that a "roadblock"—an advertising term for a full-page advertisement in major newspapers across the nation—conducted through the American Newspaper Publishers Association during the Memorial Day weekend in 1999 was extremely effective in generating contributions. Such was the cross-generational appeal of the campaign that the ABMC received a letter from Fayetteville, New York, addressed to Tom Hanks, which opened with:

> *Dear Mr. Hanks,*
> *My name is Zane Fayos. I am ten years old. I have saved $195. My mother showed me your ad in the newspaper about the National World War II Memorial and I decided that I would like to give my money to help build the memorial.*

The young lad continued on to discuss how he loved to build model airplanes, his favorite movie was *Memphis Belle*, and that he had become an avid reader of books about D-Day, noting that his mother had promised that he could someday see the film *Saving Private Ryan*. Fayos concluded with:

> *Do you know when the memorial will be built and what it will look like? I hope to go to Washington, D.C., to see the memorial when it is finished. I hope this money helps.*
> *Your Friend,*
> *Zane Fayos*

The elevated level of visibility provided by Hanks helped other facets of fundraising, such as direct mail. Whereas in fiscal year 1998 it had cost the campaign fifty-one cents to raise each dollar in contribution, during the 1999 fiscal year that cost had dropped to twenty-six cents per dollar.[4]

The campaign communications director, Colonel Conley, recalled that having an approved memorial design also helped the cause: "We could show people what their donated dollars were going to buy."[5]

As the needed funding came in, that design continued to evolve.

Chapter Seven

THE EVOLVING DESIGN

1998–99

Throughout the summer and fall of 1998, the SDC met with the St.Florian design team, both to make refinements to the approved design and attempt to wrap their arms around content. In a memorandum sent from Helen Fagin to Haydn Williams in mid-July she reminded the ambassador, "We are charged with telling a multifaceted story" and subsequently listed a number of thematic story lines that the new memorial needed to communicate to the public. Williams partially agreed. Writing back, he concurred on the need for a content visions paper for St.Florian and his consultant Edwin Schlossberg. However, he pushed back a bit, noting that the intent of the legislation authorizing the memorial was to honor those who had served in the armed forces and the nation's participation in the war—"That is all." He reminded Fagin that the SDC had broadened the purpose of the memorial but, "We can't simply tell 'a multifaceted story'" covering the components she had proposed in any detail. He cited Benjamin Forgey, who had earlier written that "the memorial should be a shrine, not a school." Having stated that, Williams agreed on the need for a unifying concept vision and visitor experience concepts, to some organization and structure in the final product and to facilitate the recommendations that had been made by the Brown- and Gantt-led commissions. He then tasked Fagin with drafting a concept guidance paper for presentation at the forthcoming SDC meeting to be held in September.[1]

Having spent the month of August in Italy, St.Florian returned to find that a detailed memorandum full of action items from Williams awaited his attention. Besides asking the architect to complete his schematic designs by the first quarter of 1999—"sooner if possible"—Williams passed along schematic design considerations based on CFA and NCPC suggestions. One idea Williams asked St.Florian to look at was the Feldman recommendation of an amphitheater. Another suggestion was to reshape the memorial arches to incorporate metal over granite. Citing Helen Fagin, Williams added, "From now on every element of the memorial's design *should be content sensitive and content friendly*."[2]

On the evening of September 15, Williams hosted the SDC for dinner at the Cosmos Club. He invited Schlossberg and Earl A. "Rusty" Powell, the National Gallery of Art director, to break bread and to conduct some advance discussions for the next day's meeting, which featured a packed agenda. The next morning began with a presentation by Barry Owenby. Recently hired by the ABMC to serve as the World War II Memorial Project executive, the Citadel graduate came over from GSA, where he had served as a senior procurement official and contracts manager. Representing the agency chartered by Congress to build the memorial, Owenby briefed the attendees on the relationships between the ABMC, the GSA, Leo A. Daly, and St.Florian and his design team.

During the ensuing discussions, Williams achieved an understanding that "the role of the SDC was to provide the lead designer with vision, guidance, and encouragement, that it was to function on an ad referendum basis as needed." It was further agreed that the designer should be given the necessary freedom to use his or his team's full creative talents, with the understanding that they would be receptive and responsive to the committee's ideas and broad guidance.

As the morning progressed, the group discussed the work schedule and Williams set a target date of January 7, 1999, to produce schematic drawings suitable for CFA and NCPC review. As for what would go into those drawings, the group reviewed some of the recommendations and found consensus that the amphitheater inclusion would alter the character of the design. However, Williams asked that Feldman's idea be studied further. Suggestions for western access into the memorial were discussed, as opponents argued that the westside back wall of the St.Florian design blocked east-west pedestrian traffic along the Mall. St.Florian stated such access was doable and would later produce drawings to show how it could be done. Reflecting two decades later, St.Florian regrets not having direct passageways between the memorial's Rainbow Pool area and the Lincoln Memorial Reflecting Pool. In the end, St.Florian argued that the NPS would oppose the passages because they did not want to allow tourists direct access to the Reflecting Pool, where they could trample on the adjacent grass. St.Florian also proposed "The Light of Freedom." Unveiling a small model, St.Florian's idea of light triumphant over darkness intrigued the attendees, who gave him the go-ahead to further develop the concept.[3]

Three weeks later, on October 9 in New York City at the offices of Hugh Hardy, Williams invited St.Florian to conduct a mini-charette to discuss potential solutions to challenges posed at the September 16 SDC gathering. In addition to Hardy, the CFA's J. Carter Brown and Frederick Lindstrom, GSA chief architect Ed Feiner, and Fagin and Williams of the SDC were present to serve as a sounding board for St.Florian's ideas. Since they were in the Big Apple, Williams and Fagin subsequently visited Edwin Schlossberg and his staff to further discuss content development.[4]

Returning to his Providence studios, St.Florian opened a letter from Judith Scott Feldman pitching the idea of incorporating into his design rocks from actual battlefields from around the globe: "It could help make the past present," she wrote, noting that "there is enormous literature in museum studies dealing with objects and why visitors want to see, touch, and simply be around things which have their own history." The professor who twice came to public hearings to oppose St.Florian's designs concluded, "Friedrich, I shall leave you to your work, Thank you for your time." After her signature she added the handwritten note, "I hope all is well with you."[5]

St.Florian brought the letter with him to share with the SDC when he returned to the nation's capital on October 13, where he joined with Williams to call on Rusty Powell at the National Gallery of Art. Powell encouraged the architect to create a work of art and agreed to serve as a pro bono adviser to the project. Williams and St.Florian made additional calls to brief local officials the next day and then convened the SDC on October 15. In addition to Pat Foote, Rolly Kidder, and Helen Fagin, Williams invited Ming Chang from the MAB and Gail Reals from the ABMC to join in. Besides hearing a progress report from St.Florian, the retired Navy rear admiral and Marine Corps brigadier general heard a presentation from Edwin Schlossberg representing Edwin Schlossberg Incorporated (ESI).[6]

Presenting his preliminary content development study, Schlossberg made eleven recommendations. Some suggestions—such as having an orientation assembly area, layering the home front narrative with the overseas story, designating the north and south memorial arches as victory in the Atlantic and victory in the Pacific, having the fountains below the arches represent victory at sea, and including the allies—earned the support of Williams and the others. However, other recommendations sounded good but fell short on specifics. Next to Schlossberg's recommendations to have visitors follow a sequence, to differentiate the narrative on entry and exit, and to make the entry a threshold, Williams wrote, "How?" Schlossberg argued that the memorial needed a voice. Williams agreed but jotted, "What's that voice?" Schlossberg recommended boundaries for content. Williams wrote down, "Yes, but define." Finally, regarding a Schlossberg recommendation for a section depicting the horrors of war, Williams had serious questions on the scope.

Schlossberg made some additional recommendations to include incorporating "sacred" stones from the overseas ABMC cemeteries into the walls of the
memorial, a recommendation that caused Chang, Kidder, and Fagin to wince,
because the number of boulders would cause clutter. Schlossberg offered the
idea of making small stones available for placement against the pillars representing the states and territories, providing visitors a way to pay homage to
those back home who had fallen in the cause of freedom. Rolly Kidder understood that the concept followed the Jewish tradition of leaving stones instead
of flowers at grave sites; however, he worried that the majority of the general
public would not make that connection. Others worried that the stones could
also be thrown. Not making much headway, Schlossberg unveiled the "Ceremony of Light" concept of having 408 floodlights (each representing one thousand American fatalities) shine up into the Washington sky. Kidder and Fagin
were aghast. Pat Foote labeled it "Hollywood comes to town" and feared it
would be harshly mocked by critics.[7]

In the ensuing correspondence, Kidder wrote, "Overall I'm not impressed
with the proposals." Foote agreed. "To put it bluntly, I believe ESI totally
missed the mark." In her feedback to Williams, Fagin included an observation
of the Feldman letter that St.Florian had shared: "Whether or not one would
agree with her concept, it is refreshing to note that she came forward with
some original ideas. I was especially touched by her imaginative approach to
symbolism, something I had not been able to discern in any of Schlossberg's
presentations."

As for a forthcoming anticipated revised proposal from ESI, Fagin wrote,
"I would love to be pleasantly surprised."[8]

There was no SDC meeting in November. Instead, the committee and
St.Florian spent a weekend participating in a joint meeting of the ABMC and
the MAB to celebrate the seventy-fifth anniversary of the former organization's founding. Williams spent time briefing his fellow commissioners and
advisory board members. In turn, Williams sat in on presentations from Barry
Owenby, who estimated the smaller design would now cost $88.7 million to

build—some $20 million less than the original proposal. Jim Aylward announced the formation of a Rose "Rosie the Riveter" Monroe Society to generate support for the home front aspect of the memorial. Mike Conley discussed public affairs and a "grassroots" kit developed by Burson-Marsteller, and unveiled a campaign logo incorporating the memorial arch. To his dismay, the SDC members in attendance rejected the concept. General Woerner invited new suggestions.[9]

The SDC also proved dismissive the following month, when they met to discuss the revised November 17 edition of the ESI proposal and concluded that Schlossberg had failed to produce the desired content vision. Schlossberg was subsequently informed and released from the project. In contrast, St.Florian offered some ideas about the memorial arches that generated a more upbeat response.

Reflecting back two decades later, St.Florian recalled feeling pressure from "the generals"—those retired military commissioners with the ABMC and MAB—to have the memorial be more celebratory of the victory. The architect recalled a conversation where one of the former commissioned officers had asked about installing something similar to the Nelson column at Trafalgar Square—only larger. St.Florian thought to himself, "Who are we going to stick up on top? Patton?"

To acknowledge the triumph of American armed forces, St.Florian envisioned suspending a large ten-foot diameter wreath from within each memorial arch. The engineering challenge proved to be weight. Worried that the granite structure alone would be incapable of handling the load, St.Florian played with the concept of incorporating steel into the design. For example, in one of the drawings he produced, the arches looked similar to the top portion of the George Washington Bridge spanning the Hudson River between New York and New Jersey. It was Ray Kaskey who came to the rescue, using the concept of a baldachino based on an installation he had seen in a chapel in Rome. St.Florian recalled, "Ray came up with such a brilliant idea overnight, with the four eagles perched on four columns with flowing ribbons in their beaks." The SDC concurred with the interior concept, though felt St.Florian still had a way to go on the arches themselves, which were described as "boxy and bulky." Yet, a lot had been accomplished in 1998 in advancing the design of the World War II Memorial.[10]

As for the pillars, the committee seemed fixated on alternating shields and laurel wreaths. Within a sacred precinct located along the west side, the idea of a rough black granite surface under a flame of freedom had taken traction. By this time Williams realized he was not going to have the drawings he desired to meet his earlier deadline of January 7 of the new year.

Williams convened a "rump" session of the SDC on January 29, 1999. Writing to St.Florian afterward, Williams still expressed dissatisfaction on the shape of the arches. As for the pillars, the ambassador reported that the group remained split on square or circular columns but were showing a preference for the latter. For adorning the pillars, St.Florian was now asked to consider alternating wreaths and eagles. Williams also instructed St.Florian to incorporate a cenotaph in the design, recommending he use the cenotaph at the ABMC Oise-Aisne cemetery in France as a model.[11]

Having traveled to the ABMC cemeteries overseas, and with Arlington Cemetery just across the Potomac, St.Florian didn't care for the suggested cemetery-appropriate cenotaph component, since he saw the central themes as national unity and the celebration of liberty and freedom. However, the architect worked to mollify the client by having his design team produce drawings depicting the SDC-suggested alterations.[12]

Returning from the late January meeting, Helen Fagin fell ill, but remained engaged. In a note to Williams drafted on Groundhog Day, she wrote, "Haydn, I'm writing this while still in the hospital, hopefully I'll be released tomorrow and allowed to recuperate under Sidney's loving care." Thanking Williams for his concerns and phone calls, she then drafted a laundry list of issues that she argued needed to be tackled.[13]

Williams was mindful of that laundry list when the SDC again met on February 8. Decisions were reached to pave the complete plaza area with granite, instead of planting grass in portions, and to eliminate the concept of six service flagpoles to fly the flags of each service in favor of two large poles that would each fly the Stars and Stripes. The debate continued on how to adorn the pillars. Rusty Powell and his staff favored placing shields over state and territory emblems. Ray Kaskey liked the alternating wreath and eagle scheme. With the solution still to be reached, Williams met privately with J. Carter Brown and Rusty Powell before returning to San Francisco. He learned that Powell was more supportive of the wreaths than his staff. "Brown is of the same mind," he recorded. Brown would poll his fellow CFA commissioners for their thoughts.[14]

To St.Florian, the indecision and repeated requests to go back to the drawing board took a toll. James S. Russell, the editor-at-large for *Architectural Record*, could discern some of St.Florian's frustration during a visit to the Providence studio, when he glanced around to see stacks of drawings and models depicting rejected ideas. Regarding the revised design, St.Florian expressed concern that a World War II veteran had told him his revised design "was too pastoral" and that World War II was "no walk in the park." In his piece published in the *New York Times* on April 4, 1999, "Art and Politics Vie In a Battle to Honor A Monumental War," Russell cited St.Florian and Kaskey attempting to reestablish the evocative experience of the original design, gestures that Russell warned could be undercut by the various federal commissions overseeing the project. Noting demands that the inscriptions and allegorical sculptures "must thank the allies, the home front, each branch of the armed services, and so on," Russell feared, "With this architectural equivalent of an Academy Awards acceptance speech, it will be difficult for the memorial to convey the immensity and deep significance of the event."[15]

While the Russell piece likely fell on deaf ears with regard to St.Florian's overseers, it should be noted that the ABMC commissioners, at their 127th meeting held on April 27, accepted a proposal from the SDC that St.Florian's preliminary design should be forwarded to the CFA and NCPC for approval. Progress was being made. In addition, the commissioners learned that another design had been approved—that for a World War II Memorial Campaign logo. Initially a blue box that had contained the words "World War II Memorial," the graphic designers at Burson-Marsteller took the liberty to insert the word "National" in the box atop of World War II.[16]

The commissioners also took note that Congressman Bob Stump of Arizona, the chair of the Veterans Affairs Committee, had drafted legislation—H.R. 1247: The World War II Memorial Completion Act—to allow the campaign to borrow money from the treasury, to meet the 1986 Commemorative Works Act requirement that all funds be on hand before any construction could occur. Williams underlined that the act extended the ABMC's authority to construct the memorial until December 31, 2005. With veterans continuing to pass away at a rate of one thousand a day, the ambassador had no intention of taking advantage of the extra time provided.[17]

At the ABMC gathering, Williams met with Francis B. "Frank" Moore, who had been appointed to the commission the previous November. He filled a vacancy left by the departure of commissioner Edward L. Romero, who had been confirmed as the next U.S. ambassador to Spain. Raised in rural Georgia, Moore had attended the University of Georgia and served in the Georgia Air National Guard. The young man subsequently interviewed for an executive director position with a recently created rural planning commission. The chair of the commission, a former naval officer and peanut farmer named Jimmy Carter, hired him. Subsequently Moore followed Carter as he claimed the governor's mansion and then edged out Gerald Ford in 1976 to become the thirty-ninth president of the United States. Moore's job in the new administration as the director of Congressional Relations meant that he was Carter's point man on the Hill to seek passage of legislation supporting the administration's objectives. Given his résumé, Moore was surprised when Williams invited him to join the SDC. Though he had no architectural background, Moore had an astute ability to observe and good common sense that would serve the committee well . . . and he possessed skill sets that would prove invaluable at a later date.[18]

On May 20, the CFA held a hearing to review the improved design concept. Ambassador Williams and Friedrich St.Florian gave lengthy updates about how the design had evolved. Once again, Judith Scott Feldman, representing the Committee of 100, spoke out in opposition, arguing that the latest St.Florian iteration was inferior to the previous two. She expressed dismay at the inclusion of the cenotaph, which she labeled a sarcophagus, saying that it gave the site the feel of a cemetery. Reflecting the concern from the Russell piece, she worried that additional elements being inserted were making the final design too complex.[19]

The Brown-led commission, having been totally engaged in the evolving design, voted unanimously to accept the progress to date. With the NCPC hearing scheduled for early June, both sides targeted Harvey Gantt. Architect David Childs wrote to the NCPC chair that the revised direction St.Florian had taken "recaptures the restrained power of the original competition entry." In contrast, Gantt received a missive from Judith Scott Feldman stating that "it has become a veritable museum for war." Feldman then recommended shoving the memorial back to the Constitution Gardens site and using the Rainbow Pool to quench and nourish the National Mall. Following the hearing, which replicated the presentations made two weeks earlier before the CFA, the NCPC also voted to allow the ABMC and St.Florian to complete their design work.

Chapter Eight

COMPLETING THE DESIGN

1999–2000

URING THE SUMMER of 1999, Fagin wrote to Williams to discuss a recent stroll she had taken along the Mall in and around the vicinity of the Rainbow Pool. Looking at the Franklin D. Roosevelt Memorial, she thought, "What kind of story will our memorial contain?" Reading on, Williams underlined her observations from the Rainbow Pool: "Awestruck by the majesty of this view, I realized what a great responsibility we have to the nation in making sure that the World War II Memorial would not diminish this grandeur." She continued, "And soon I realized that this place is not about the glorification of war, but about the ideas and achievements that emerged from the nation's commitment to ideals and democracy." Again, Williams broke out his pencil to underline: "This is a memorial to the American spirit and to the sacrifices Americans made to secure for themselves and for others the freedom of living in a democracy." Fagin's letter continued on to discuss the conceptual components of St. Florian's revised design, looking at the symbolic meaning of the arches and the ceremonial plaza. Williams again could not resist his urge to underline: "A cenotaph says it all—it is a symbolic resting place on American soil in the nation's capital for the more than 400,000 soldiers who never came home." Fagin concluded, "Finally an image of hope—the Torch of Freedom." These last two heavily symbolic features would not make the final cut.[1]

Whereas St.Florian may have been annoyed with some of the quibbling on aspects of his design from the SDC, there were design aspects of the memorial on which he was more than happy to obtain guidance. For example, assigning state names to pillars. St.Florian sat back and watched the Williams-led panel discuss the merits of alphabetical order versus state size, and so forth. Today, visitors will note that the state names on the pillars are based on their date of admission to the Union, starting with Delaware and Pennsylvania and alternating outward from the sacred precinct.[2]

Williams continued to gather the SDC monthly to review a long checklist of decision and action items provided by architects at Leo A. Daly, who were working with the St.Florian-led design team. Following the August SDC meeting held just prior to the commissioners' meeting, Williams wrote a critique to St.Florian suggesting that he take another look at the visitor flow, and expressing concern that the flagpoles for service flags would have to fall by the wayside due to National Park Service concerns. Williams then penned out additional comments, which were then translated onto six typed pages for the winning architect to consider.

Meanwhile, debate about the evolving design and the location of the memorial continued to ferment within architectural circles and "unofficial Washington." Though Judith Scott Feldman had earned support from the chairman of the Committee of 100, Tersh Boasberg, and several colleagues, not all on the committee shared her harsh critique of the World War II Memorial project. Responding to one of Feldman's attacks on the St.Florian design, Washington College architecture professor Richard Striner, a member of the committee, wrote to Feldman, "Your letter was so offensive," and objected to the characterization of the proposed memorial as "Fascist reminiscent." In his rebuke, Striner aligned with the *Boston Globe* critic Bob Campbell in arguing that the plans fit more into the New Deal architectural genre. Feldman defended herself in a five-page heavily footnoted letter, citing the teachings of several architects who had influenced her worldview. Striner wrote back, "I have reviewed your arguments carefully. Having done so I must tell you in my opinion that you have utterly failed to refute my objections to your position on the World War II Memorial."[3]

Williams and Brown collaborated to exploit the internal dissension. On October 8, J. Carter Brown took his turn at writing a five-page missive to the Committee of 100 chairman, strongly defending the work of Williams' Site and Design Committee and the attributes of the St.Florian design and observing, "It seems the word travesty is somewhat exaggerated." Williams followed up with an offer to meet with Boasberg in November. The cordial outreach to the opposition leadership failed to make any headway. Indeed, opponents of the memorial could only be buoyed when the *Washington Post* reported a joint task force on memorials consisting of members of the CFA, NCPC, and NCMC had recommended a "no build zone" on the Mall regarding future memorial proposals. Though the World War II Memorial would not be affected, the recommendation supported an opposition narrative that the Mall was a sacred area that should not be altered.[4]

Progress advanced enough on the design to start the conversation on materials. Following their established regimen of a Friday night dinner at the Cosmos Club, the SDC met on the last Saturday of October in 1999 at the architectural offices of Leo A. Daly to start a multiday working session. For that first day, noted Dallas architectural critic David Dillon joined in the conversation, since granite was the topic de jour. St.Florian provided a one-day tutorial on the substance that varied depending on where it was quarried and cut. On the following day, the group took a morning Halloween tour around the city to study how granite had been used throughout the nation's capital on various plazas and structures. Returning to the Leo A. Daly meeting room in the afternoon, the SDC were provided with granite samples to examine. The weekend concluded with a working dinner. As the calendar turned to

November, the Williams team adjourned to Leo A. Daly's and, following an executive session, called in St.Florian and his design team to cover a set-in-stone agenda for the morning to decide on granite selection, followed by an afternoon conversation on a monument marker to represent sacrifice. By this time, the cenotaph idea had fallen out of favor (much to St.Florian's delight), a victim of opposition claims that the SDC intended to build a giant sarcophagus on the Mall—a misrepresentation that took a poignant design solution out of play. The Light of Freedom concept remained viable, as did the idea of having a broken plane feature in the Rainbow Pool. St.Florian latched on to the idea of incorporating gold stars into the memorial plaza floor. Williams winced at the suggestion. With each star representing hundreds if not thousands of Americans killed, the concept gave the perception that visitors would be stepping on the graves of the dead. During an "Ah ha!" moment, it was suggested that perhaps the stars could be mounted on the western wall between the Reflecting Pool and the plaza surrounding the Rainbow Pool.[5]

In the wake of the early November gatherings, Leo A. Daly liaison John Hart sent Williams a memorandum titled "Critical Decisions." It listed the priorities that needed to be addressed if a final design were to be approved in time for a projected groundbreaking ceremony scheduled for Veterans Day a mere year away. Among the issues yet to be decided were the significant architectural elements that aimed to commemorate sacrifice, paving patterns, content locations, lighting, water fountain features, inscriptions, and bas reliefs. Reinforcing a point previously made by Helen Fagin, Hart wrote, "We still haven't determined what story we are telling." In response, Williams provided an update that several of these issues were being addressed and underlined, "We are not looking for a way to delay and prolong decisions on content. On the other hand, the client does not want to be put in a position where content is determined by construction schedules or other arbitrary dates set for the future." Rolly Kidder recalled that Williams shared with him the same sentiments, noting that the ABMC staff constantly reminded him of the ticking clock: "The staff keeps saying 'The Russians are coming! The Russians are coming!'—That's crap! We've got time to get this thing done right." However, in his memo Williams did confess, "With 365 days to go to November 11, 2000, we have our work cut out for us." Hart wrote back to remind Williams: "Regarding the stone pattern and dimensions for walls, Friedrich is the designer and has the responsibility for making such decisions." Recognizing that the SDC had reserved final judgment, Hart urged resolutions, because delayed decisions on such features as fountains affected how lighting was to be placed. To help with the process, Hart urged Williams to prioritize, since issues dealing with landscaping and ancillary buildings could be addressed at a later date. [6]

The early December gathering of the SDC made headway in addressing some of the issues. St.Florian recalled privately meeting with Williams just prior to the SDC gathering, to preview some of the drawings, and on this trip he brought with him a large rendering of the concept proposed at the previous meeting to have gold stars mounted vertically on a granite background. Williams just stared at the drawing. St.Florian recounted, "I could see he was over-come with emotion, so I left the room. After a few minutes when I came back into the room, he was still looking at the stars, and there were tears in his eyes. He said nothing, then shook my hand and wiped the tears from his eyes. It was a very powerful moment for both of us."[7]

As with the late October/early November meeting, a bus tour was incor-porated into the agenda—this time at night, to view how the various monu-ments and memorials in Washington were lit. Agreement was reached to place the two large flagpoles at the two walkways coming in from 17th Street, repli-cating the flag arrangement at Union Station. Service flags could be brought in for ceremonies. The committee also shared Williams' positive reaction to the concept of having the ceremonial sacred area centered on a wall on which were mounted gold stars representing those who had made the ultimate sacrifice. Left to be determined was how many souls each star would represent. Also to be determined was the Light of Freedom. ABMC had commissioned several noted sculptors in a mini competition to create the illustrative piece. Noted architect-sculptor Kent Bloomer came down from Yale to share two concepts he had developed as a potential solution. One design featured a crucible emerging from a crater, with bronze and gold sculpted flames and a small flame atop. Bloomer then offered an abstract design of a ray of lights radiating out from a crucible rising from the proposed broken plane. The committee made no commitment to either design. Noted minimalist Frank Stella's entry consisted of a modern conglomeration of twisted steel. Rolly Kidder recalled J. Carter Brown saying, "Isn't it wonderful? It reminds me of St. George slaying the dragon," and Haydn Williams responding, "It looks to me like a busted-up shopping cart."

With such differing artistic tastes, no Light of Freedom sculpture would ever be commissioned. However, the SDC did approve the Ray Kaskey balustrade design to join the individual pillars representing states and territories with a bronze rope. The initial design had the rope carved from stone. Frank Moore, who along with Pat Foote had been tasked by Williams to form the "rope" subcommittee, gave credit to Ray Kaskey for the idea of casting the rope in bronze, a concept endorsed by Brown. Brown would eventually push the idea of having the bronze ropes be freestanding rather than having them framed in stone.[8] Kaskey and Bloomer also recommended that the bas reliefs not be life size. Agreement would eventually be reached to maintain the same scale for each of the reliefs.

Writing to Williams in the wake of the December gathering, Helen Fagin once again addressed the issue of what story the memorial would tell. Acknowledging plans to install a series of bas reliefs, Fagin reemphasized the inscriptions, "They must contain the strongest and impactful language." Overall though, Fagin was pleased with the progress that had been made closing her letter with, "Haydn, I wish to congratulate you on the effectiveness of your leadership during the meetings last weekend. You worked us hard, but still, you worked harder than any of us. You truly lead by example. I am honored to serve under your guidance and brilliant leadership."

During the holiday season, which included millennial celebrations that featured concerts and fireworks centered on the Lincoln Memorial, St.Florian and his design team implemented the decisions made during the early

December meetings for presentation at the next SDC meeting scheduled for January 17 in the new year. In an e-mail to Helen Fagin a week prior to the meeting, David Dillon supported her concern on the storytelling aspect: "It is critical that we spend a good deal of time on the inscription issue over the weekend deciding the which and the where and the how. We don't have a lot of time left."[9]

Once again, the SDC gathered in the conference room at the headquarters of Leo A. Daly on the Martin Luther King Jr. weekend to finalize decisions on the dimensions of the plaza, the level below ground of the Rainbow Pool, and the height of both the arches and the wall that would host the gold stars. The addition of coral gray and green granite to the plaza was approved. The tops of the arches were modified to make them conform with the pillar tops. Small refinements were made on the north and south baldachinos.[10] A significant decision finally reached was to adorn each of the fifty-six pillars with two sculpted bronze wreaths, with one depicting oak leaves and the other wheat spears, alternating front and back. "The oak symbolizes the industrial might of the nation—the arsenal of democracy. The wheat represents the agricultural power of the nation—the breadbasket of the world."[11] Again, St.Florian marveled at the group-think process of the SDC that led to this outcome. Should the type of wreath assigned to a pillar corollate to whether a state or territory is predominantly industrial or agricultural? If not, then just alternating wreaths may mean that a predominantly agricultural state such as Iowa might be adorned with an oak wreath. Ultimately, the alternating front and back solution solved the problem and recognized that all states and territories contributed both agricultural and industrial goods.[12]

The SDC agreed that there would be twenty-four bas reliefs flanking the entrance area that led to the plaza surrounding the Rainbow Pool. As for the content, that decision would be deferred to a later date along with what inscriptions to cut into the stone. More pressing from a nonaesthetical standpoint was the capacity to pump water to the fountains and waterfalls. The initial vision was to place the mechanical vault beneath a comfort station located some four hundred feet southwest of the memorial. However, at the close of January, John Hart wrote to Williams that the engineers at Leo A. Daly had ceased work on the comfort station plans, citing the scale of pressure needed at that distance to force water up through the various nozzles. Ultimately the mechanical vault would be placed beneath the memorial itself.[13]

Another element that brought about unanticipated aesthetic and technical challenges was the Light of Freedom. Apparently not enamored with the various torch design submissions, the committee drafted a request for a proposal calling for a torch to rise from dark stone, from either the center of the Rainbow Pool or adjacent to the field of gold stars. Williams was intrigued with the eternal flame concept, having frequently witnessed the glow at night of the flame at the Kennedy graves at Arlington Cemetery while driving across the Memorial Bridge. Unfortunately for Williams, the flame concept received a dose of reality when he received a memorandum from Hart with the subject line "Use of Gas Flame," covering the costs of natural gas, environmental impacts, safety, and maintenance. Looking at the pros and cons, he found a lot of cons. The first challenge was getting gas to the site. True, there was a gas line under 17th street. However, that was a high-pressure line unsuitable for tapping. The nearest low-pressure line that could provide a feed was at 20th Street. The estimated cost of running a line from that source was $1 million. Anticipating a query on using propane, Hart reported that a 1,000-gallon tank would have to be replenished every fifteen days. Other concerns that Hart relayed included potential damage, over the long term, of memorial materials due to the flame exhaust, as well as concerns expressed by the National Park Service that the flame would serve as a magnet for the homeless on cold evenings.[14]

Given the costs and effort to pursue such an option, Williams and J. Carter Brown drove to Gettysburg to look at the Paul Cret–designed Eternal Light Peace Memorial. Dedicated on July 3, 1938, by President Franklin D. Roosevelt in a ceremony that drew more than a quarter million Americans to mark the seventy-fifth anniversary of that pivotal battle, the flame burned atop a

47½-foot-high shaft featuring granite from Maine and Alabama. Ray Kaskey recalled that Williams returned to report he could not see the torch during daylight. The World War II Memorial would *not* feature a burning flame.[15]

On paper, there was just one SDC meeting in mid-February. However, Williams and fellow commissioners serving on the SDC needed to return to Washington on February 29 for the 129th commissioners' meeting of the ABMC. For General Woerner's group, the news was upbeat about the design and fundraising. As of the end of January, the campaign had raised approximately $82 million. Most impressive was the diversity of sources. Corporations had donated some $28 million through direct contributions—90 percent of the goal. Some 357,000 individual donors had nearly matched that number thanks to direct mail and appeals over a rapidly evolving Internet. The aforementioned state campaigns and appeals to veteran groups had brought in another $15 million. As for publicity, the public service announcements had drawn more media interest than any Ad Council campaign in recent memory. A partnership with the History Channel promised a manual for grades 4 through 8 that would tie into a documentary about World War II and the building of the memorial.[16]

Yet for Haydn Williams, concerns remained that the juggernaut effort could still be stopped dead in its tracks. Having been in correspondence with the noted World War II historian Stephen Ambrose, Williams took the opportunity to bring him up from New Orleans a week before the commissioners' meeting to meet with the SDC and St. Florian's design team as well as David Childs and Maj. Gen. John Herrling. Ambrose looked over the table model of the memorial. Kidder recalled the historian's reaction, "The veterans are going to love it!" Williams jotted down comments from *The Band of Brothers* author, who saw the importance of the Light of Freedom concept. "*Light over darkness* process continues," Williams noted. Ambrose expressed concern that there was much clutter. He concurred with the growing consensus that the Light of Freedom needed to be pulled away from the wall of gold stars and placed in the Rainbow Pool. As for inscriptions noting key battles, Ambrose again cited clutter and feared that, inevitably, they would leave something out—"By not naming, you are inclusive."[17]

On March 6, Williams followed up the Washington briefing of Ambrose with a phone call and followed that on the next day with a summation letter. Williams thanked Ambrose for his feedback on the model and suggestions to eliminate clutter. Then the ambassador cut to the chase. "There remains, in Washington, a small but determined and influential group that is intent on derailing what we are trying to accomplish." Williams wrote on, "Our plan is to go before the federal approval authorities in June and July with the final design plan including content." Williams then asked Ambrose if he would be willing to chair the final World War II Memorial panel to meet sometime that spring. Ambrose wrote back he would be willing to come up in mid-April.[18]

Williams had reason for concern. Judith Scott Feldman continued to associate the St.Florian design with Hitler's Germany: "When those pillars went up with those wreaths, with the coffin as the centerpiece and there was an eternal flame in the sacred precinct, I could not help thinking of the Nazis." With dissension to that contention within the Committee of 100, Feldman led the charge to form a nonprofit, the National Coalition to Save Our Mall, to focus on defeating the effort to use the Rainbow Pool site for the World War II Memorial.[19]

At both the March and April SDC meetings with St.Florian's design team, elements of the design were massaged. The concept of a north and south fountain in the Rainbow Pool was approved. A contention arose with the National Park Service over the ranger station to be built to the south of the memorial. The NPS, concerned about long-term cost, desired a minimalist facility with no internal space for visitors. In contrast, the SDC desired an interior space that could house a gift shop and bookstore as well as restrooms. In the end, the ABMC would have to settle for a 370-square-foot information station. Restrooms would be made available in a separate structure.[20]

With two months to go before their presentation to the CFA for its blessing on a final plan, the SDC finally began to address the storytelling components of the memorial. The production of twenty-four bas reliefs had been approved. The advisory group led by Ambrose would assist in determining the subjects for those reliefs. Regarding the selection of inscriptions to be carved into the various blank surfaces of granite, Williams realized he needed help in first identifying the available verbiage. As a result of informal liaisons between Williams and members of Senator Inouye's staff, in mid-April the senator received a formal request from the ABMC to ask the Library of Congress to research quotes from "Statesmen, FDR, Truman, Churchill, American military leaders, war correspondents, writers, historians, citizen soldiers, patriots serving on the homefront, the poet. We are looking for words that speak to the following themes: national unity during World War II, the Spirit of America, the homefront, the arsenal of democracy, the valor of our combat arms, the victory won, the cost of sacrifice, and finally—the legacy of war. Brevity is important. Suggest a deadline of May 19."[21]

Inouye subsequently forwarded the request to Librarian of Congress James Billington. As the Library of Congress staffers rose to the challenge of scouring hundreds of speeches, books, recordings, and other assorted media to uncover quotes suitable for permanent fixture in granite, Williams pushed ahead, now convening his group twice a month to finalize details. Landscape now came into focus as James van Sweden discussed floral and shrubbery plans. Much of van Sweden's work dealt with the exterior areas of the memorial. An initial vision van Sweden attempted to sell was to surround the exterior areas with white rose bushes. Kidder remembered, "The park service said 'No'—the prickers and thorns would deter park workers from picking up garbage." One feature addressed in early May was the Circle of Remembrance. The concept was to create a quiet space for veterans and their families to rest and reflect. Van Sweden proposed this contemplative area to be set to the northwest of the memorial, an enclosed circle of benches overlooking the pond setting of the Constitution Gardens.[22]

Besides reviewing landscaping, the May SDC working group gatherings looked at a number of issues, ranging from placing the service seals on the base of the flagpoles to how the gold stars would be constructed and fitted onto the wall of remembrance. Of note, much discussion focused on how to mount banners on the pillars for ceremonial occasions.[23] Just prior to the SDC Working Group meeting on May 20, Williams attended a small reception at the Library of Congress hosted by Judith Prowess Reid, who had led the quotation search project. In his thank-you letter, Williams noted, "Gary Wills has written that words are a more powerful preservative of history than marble or bronze and that we assume a burden when we labor a monument into being." To reemphasize the great service performed by her staff, Williams added, "What we choose to remember in stone tells us who we are or want to be."[24]

Despite or perhaps because of the full court press to get a full design before the CFA for its June hearing, the SDC simply ran out of time. Too many issues still needed resolution, and discussions during the working group deliberations often resurrected issues that had been thought resolved earlier. Unfortunately for the ABMC, by not getting on the CFA docket until late July gave the opposition, whom J. Carter Brown had once dismissed as "cabal of messianic detractors," more time to rally. For the National Coalition to Save Our Mall, the message was not to oppose the concept of the memorial—all agreed the Greatest Generation was owed recognition—but that the location was inappropriate. Thus, Judith Scott Feldman turned to John Graves to serve as the face of the media campaign launched on June 5, which aimed to change public support for the project. The World War II veteran, who had spoken against the memorial location in earlier hearings, appeared in television advertising where he pleaded against the plan that his coalition argued would pave over the Mall. Responding to the multifaceted attack launched by Feldman's group, Senator Dole argued that such opposition should have made itself known earlier and it simply was too late. On June 6, the fifty-sixth anniversary of D-Day, the *Washington Post* ran Dole's op-ed piece titled "One Final Salute."[25]

With the CFA hearing scheduled for July 20, the 130th commissioners' meeting of the ABMC, held on June 27–28, provided a good sounding board for Williams and his team for the forthcoming hearing. A key component of that presentation would be a video of David Childs extolling the design of the future landmark, produced by Burson-Marsteller. Over the previous weeks, the PR firm and Williams had exchanged repeated faxes as the SDC committee chair edited, reedited, and again edited the proposed script. Williams and St.Florian spent ninety minutes briefing the commission on the near-completed design. Looking ahead, the group discussed the forthcoming groundbreaking ceremony. Jess Hay and fellow MAB member Governor Ned McWherter volunteered to serve as the cochairs of the ad hoc groundbreaking committee. The discussion then turned to the distant future. Senator Dole had recently collected a check for $14.5 million from Walmart, then the largest employer of World War II veterans in the nation with some 7,500 employees, mostly in their seventies and eighties, serving mostly as greeters. Of the Walmart contribution, $5 million came from the Walmart Foundation and the rest from donations from customers and employees who responded to the Tom Hanks kiosks that were placed in each store. With additional such bequests in the offing, the question started to become how much surplus would the fundraising campaign generate? The commissioners studied a point paper, drafted by the ABMC attorney Bill Aileo, on the concept of setting up an endowment and a foundation to support the World War II Memorial. The ideas received a tepid reception by some of the commissioners, Williams among them. The ambassador jotted to himself that legislation was already being drafted to establish an endowment for maintenance in the U.S. Treasury. He asked himself, "Who would run that?" Besides maintenance, there would be a need for commemoration programs, educational programs, and security. He then noted to himself that if ABMC retained control of the funds, ABMC could make the rules and regulations and perhaps administer a grant program. However, others on the commission and staff opted for an exit strategy upon completion that included not only turning over all responsibilities for the memorial to the NPS as dictated by the enabling legislation, but also all of the excess funds. Over time, Williams would become a founder of the not-for-profit Friends of the National World War II Memorial.[26]

As the CFA hearings approached, the debate about the memorial could be read within the pages of the *Washington Post*. On July 10, the editorial pages featured an op-ed piece in which columnist Jonathan Yardley argued that the World War II Memorial question deserved further examination. Coincidentally, the ABMC had invited the media for an open house at Leo A. Daly's, to provide an opportunity for viewing the scale models that would be presented at the forthcoming CFA hearing. Mike Conley recalled, "I'll never forget the Editorial Page editor studying the longest of the wood models, which placed the WWII Memorial in context with the Washington Monument and Lincoln Memorial. I walked up to him and he asked one question of me: 'Is this model to scale?' I simply responded: 'Yes, it is.'"

Long a supporter of the memorial, Benjamin Forgey published a piece in the *Washington Post* on July 15 titled "A Fitting Memorial in Every Way." However, the true impact of the open house became apparent the next day in the paper's Sunday editorial, which featured the banner head "Build the WWII Memorial." With CFA hearings to be held in just four days, Williams and his colleagues exuded joy when they read, "Opponents contend that the war memorial would mar one of the nation's great democratic vistas. We think they are wrong."

Four days later came the day of the CFA hearings chaired by J. Carter Brown. At the beginning of the hearing, the commissioners viewed the David Childs video and then Williams and St.Florian augmented that presentation, elaborating on the design decisions that had been made and the reasoning behind those decisions. Then came the period for public comment. For the next several hours, Brown and his colleagues heard passionate testimony for and against the memorial. Among the more vehement proponents to speak on behalf of the memorial was Brigadier General Foote. Not afraid to mix it up with Feldman and her supporters, the veteran Army officer became known in opposition circles as "That Horrible Woman."

Following six hours of public testimony, Brown polled his fellow commissioners. In the next day's *Washington Post*, Linda Wheeler reported that the

CFA had given its approval for the major elements of the design. At the end of the month, the ABMC secretary, Major General Herrling, took pleasure in writing to the commissioners of the ABMC and the members of the MAB that the CFA had voted unanimously to reaffirm its commitment to the Rainbow Pool location and to support the refined architectural design. The path to groundbreaking and ultimate construction seemed clear of obstructions.[27]

Chapter Nine

THE GROUNDBREAKING

2000

THE OUTCOME of the CFA hearing should have come as no surprise to Judith Scott Feldman and her coalition, given the strong support that J. Carter Brown had previously given to the plan in public and in private correspondence. However, while Feldman may have lost a battle, she had yet to lose the war.

A week after the CFA hearing, members of the National Coalition to Save Our Mall petitioned the D.C. Historic Preservation Review Board to terminate its ongoing consultative relationship with the ABMC and the NPS. The board declined to take that action and voted to reaffirm its support for the project.[1]

With that door slammed in its face, Feldman's group targeted the Advisory Council on Historic Preservation (ACHP). Established in 1966 with the passage of the National Historic Preservation Act, the ACHP was "an independent federal agency that promotes the preservation, enhancement, and sustainable use of our nation's diverse historic resources, and advises the President and Congress on national historic preservation policy." Three years earlier, after the site had been selected, the ACHP had written to the NPS that it would opt not to review that decision. As the design process continued, the ABMC made efforts to brief the ACHP on the evolving design, evoking little in the way of comment except for letters thanking the presenters. However, in the wake of the CFA hearing, the ACHP's executive director, John Fowler, seemed to display a case of lapsed memory when he wrote to Secretary of the Interior Bruce Babbitt to complain that the ACHP had been given too short a notice to participate in consultations on the World War II Memorial. Instead, it intended only to provide comments to the National Park Service. Apparently, the recent publicity and lobbying efforts by Feldman's group caused some members on the council to reconsider its past decision to refrain from comment. The subject was placed on the agenda for a council meeting on August 25, 2000. Informed of this development, the ABMC dispatched Rolly Kidder to read a statement arguing that the monument would enhance its surroundings. Yet on this day the opposition speakers made a more compelling case. Subsequently, the ACHP chairwoman, Cathryn Slater, wrote to Secretary Babbitt to state that the council had determined that construction of the memorial would have serious unresolvable effects on the historic character of the Mall. The September 5, 2000, letter received media attention. Two days after it was released, the headline of the Linda Wheeler piece in the *Washington Post* read, "Federal Panel Criticizes World War II Memorial."[2]

The Slater letter emboldened further opposition. In a September 15 *Wall Street Journal* editorial titled "Mauling of the Mall," the New York newspaper restated several of the Save Our Mall coalition contentions that the decision-making process had been conducted without public scrutiny.

The two shots across the bow would not go unanswered. Responding to the Slater letter, Secretary Babbitt sent the chairwoman a memorandum from Robert Stanton, the director of the National Park Service, expressing his disagreement with the ACHP finding. Haydn Williams also took the opportunity to write to Slater, reminding her that her council had passed on the opportunity to comment on the site years earlier. Williams then went after the editorial board of the *Wall Street Journal* for their "misinformed and distorted criticism," pointing out that "your article perpetuates a flawed notion about the site and design approval process" and noting that there had been seventeen public hearings on the subject since 1995.[3]

Unfortunately for Williams and the ABMC, Feldman, whose group now had a board of directors, 1,500 members, and financial backing with a $100,000 grant from the Nason Foundation, obtained copies of two 1999 studies, the first titled *Cultural Landscape Report* for the grounds surrounding West Potomac Park and the Lincoln Memorial, and the second titled *Revised National Historic Place Nominations* for East and West Potomac Parks. Obtaining the reports in July 2000, Feldman saw a passage that argued that the Reflecting Pool and Rainbow Pool were part of the historic landscape associated with the Lincoln Memorial. Such a linkage made a case that building the World War II Memorial at the Rainbow Pool site would encroach on an existing memorial— a violation of the 1986 Commemorative Works Act. Adding cannon fodder to the report finding was the appearance that the NPS had held back the reports from the public. In Washington, it's well known that the cover-up can be worse than the crime. In conflicting statements discussing the reports, their significance, and their tardy public appearance, John Parsons did not help the World War II Memorial's cause.[4]

Despite this added ammunition, the opposition failed to make their case before the National Capital Planning Commission met on September 20 to review the finalized plans for the memorial. Williams had little time to savor this public hearing victory before seeing yet another editorial in the *New York Times*, "Don't Mar the Mall," urge President Clinton to direct the ABMC to find another location. This time an aggravated Helen Fagin responded, "You are asking for the reversal of a very democratic process and by doing so impugning the judgment of all those good men and women, members of the approving commissions, who repeatedly voted overwhelmingly in favor of the present site and were diligently overseeing the process of refinement in design."[5]

Having failed to get any of the oversight commissions to change their support for the monument's location and final design, the National Coalition to

Save Our Mall filed a lawsuit in the U.S. District Court in the District of Columbia, alleging violations of the Commemorative Works Act, the National Environmental Policy Act, the National Historic Preservation Act, and the Federal Advisory Committee Act, with an aim toward blocking construction permits.

With groundbreaking scheduled less than a month away, the filing meant that the planned event would strictly be ceremonial—dirt would actually be placed into aboveground boxes for the shovels to turn over. No earthmovers would be arriving immediately thereafter. Needless to say, news of the lawsuit was not received well by the hundreds of thousands of World War II veterans and their families who had supported the fundraising campaign and had been kept abreast of the progress through the quarterly newsletters being sent out by the ABMC. In Congress, senators and representatives heard from their constituents. On October 25, Congress approved Senate Congressional Resolution 145, reaffirming bipartisan support for the World War II Memorial and the need to expedite construction.

It turned out that the fall of 2000 would be marked with even more serious litigation. The fight over the World War II Memorial occurred during a contentious presidential campaign between Vice President Al Gore and the former governor of Texas, George W. Bush. The outcome of the election could have an impact on the World War II Memorial depending on the winner. Would a President Gore support the initiative as strongly as his predecessor? Would a President Bush appoint new commissioners to the ABMC, affecting the direction of the project? The results of the November 7 election were still not determined on the day of the scheduled groundbreaking, on the eighty-second anniversary of the date marking the end of World War I. "Hanging chads" entered the national vernacular as the state of Florida conducted a recount of a vote where the Republican Bush had the slimmest of leads. The issue ultimately would be decided on December 12 in the Supreme Court. On the other hand, the World War II Memorial litigation would continue despite the congressional resolution.

Despite the question of who would be the new commander in chief clouding the official groundbreaking ceremony, President Clinton looked forward to this ceremonial event that would honor the father he never knew and the millions of others who had served alongside his dad during the most significant conflict of the twentieth century. Sadly, time continued to take its toll on the Greatest Generation. "We're a lot like the season," one veteran noted as an autumn breeze dislodged leaves from the elms lining the Mall. "We're like the leaves in that there's more of us falling each day. I'm glad I'm here to see this." One of the leaves that had fallen was Roger Durbin, who had passed away earlier that year on February 6, a victim of pancreatic cancer.[6]

The official party that arrived at 1 p.m. now consisted of Gen. Fred Woerner, Secretary of Defense William Cohen, Senator Bob Dole, Fred Smith, Ambassador Haydn Williams, Congresswoman Marcy Kaptur, Chairman Peter Wheeler, Tom Hanks, Capt. Luther Smith, Friedrich St.Florian, Jess Hay, and Archbishop Philip Hannan. Two minutes after the arrival of the official party, the Army band struck up "Hail to the Chief" as President Clinton arrived and took his place on the platform. Selected members of the official party took their turns to address the large veteran-laden gathering, which stretched across 17th St. onto the grounds of the Washington Monument.

First, General Woerner welcomed the audience and then turned the podium over to Defense Secretary Cohen. Cohen looked out at the large crowd of veterans, many in wheelchairs, and observed, "We, the heirs of your sacrifice, are citizens of the world you made and the nation you saved. We can only stand in awe at your silent courage, at your sense of duty and at the sacred gift that you have offered to all those who came after you." Representative Kaptur then took her turn at the podium. The Ohio congresswoman acknowledged the presence and service of several of her fellow legislators in attendance that day, as well as the members of the Durbin family who had come to Washington for the event. She then gave way to Luther Smith, who reflected on his service as one of the Tuskegee Airmen and recounted getting shot down over Germany and spending months in a German POW camp. Following a video presentation, Tom Hanks read a piece written by war correspondent Ernie Pyle that resonated with the audience. The campaign cochairs, Bob Dole and Fred Smith, took turns to reflect on their roles in leading the fundraising effort. Dole noted, "For some, inevitably, this memorial will be a place to mourn. For millions of others, it will be a place to learn, to reflect, and to draw inspiration for whatever tests confront generations yet unborn."[7]

The audience was then introduced to the next speaker. Perhaps Haydn Williams did not realize, as he walked to the podium, that this would mark the culminating event of his effort of six years and more to bring the World War II Memorial to fruition. The ambassador pulled out his five pages of double-spaced comments. His first page focused on thanking those who had worked with him on the SDC, and the St.Florian design team for making the design became reality. Moving on to the second page as he spoke with the Lincoln Memorial as a dramatic backdrop, Williams looked up at the Washington Monument and the Capitol beyond and praised the selection of the site as most fitting. As for discussing what was coming to that site, he dedicated his third page to lavishing praise on Friedrich St.Florian for the extraordinary effort he had made to design, and then redesign, the memorial through a deliberative process. Williams then spoke of the memorial as a gift of the American people for future generations. "When finished, the memorial will be a new and important gathering place, a place for the joyous celebration of the American spirit and national unity." Envisioning the site as a host to democratic discourse, parades, concerts, and other memorial events, the ambassador concluded by observing, "It will, in essence, be a living memorial, as well as a sacred shrine honoring the nation, the home front, the valor and sacrifice of our armed forces, our allies, and the victory won during World War II."[8]

A musical interlude then allowed the attendees to stand up and stretch after hearing the succession of remarks. Following that, President Clinton took his turn at the podium to address the veterans in the audience: "This memorial is built not only for the children whose grandparents served in the war, but for the children who will visit this place a century from now, asking questions about America's great victory for freedom." He continued, "With this memorial, we secure the memory of 16 million Americans, men and women, who took up arms in the greatest struggle humanity has ever known."[9]

Following the president's poignant remarks, fifty-six shovels were distributed to the official party, selected World War II veterans, congressional World War II veterans, and the ABMC commissioners and members of the MAB. All approached a very long trough of dirt and, on signal, thrust their shovels in and symbolically turned over the soil. "Taps" was then played with a video showing the surrender ceremony ending the war. Following a rendition of "God Bless America" and the playing of the Armed Forces Medley, where members from each of the services rose to attention when their service hymn was played, the ceremony concluded.

Unfortunately, the eloquent speeches, festivities, and good spirits associated with the faux groundbreaking ceremony did not mitigate the determination of the opposition, who had cultivated some influential friends in the media. Writing in support of Feldman's group, conservative columnist Charles Krauthammer observed, "Some causes are hopeless yet worth pursuing till the bitter end." Three days after the ceremony, Marc Fisher of the *Washington Post* wrote a scathing op-ed piece calling for halting construction. Pat Foote immediately responded at 7:40 a.m. with an e-mail to ask Fisher if he had seen the model or met with the designer. She argued that the National Coalition to Save the Mall had failed to make its case and reminded the pundit of the support of 11 million veteran members of the approximately 450 organizations that had endorsed the planned memorial. At 9:21 a.m. Fisher e-mailed back to Foote to thank her for her thoughtful note, but reaffirmed his opposition: "The more I saw of the design, the more convinced I am this will mar the Mall terribly, while leaving future generations mystified as to the true meaning and power of war." Foote contemplated that response and came to the realization she was not going to make any headway. At 4:14 p.m. she typed back, "One of the truths about building memorials in the nation's capital is such undertakings are historically controversial, frequently contentious, and always emotional." Stating the obvious, she continued, "You and I view the memorial end result through very different prisms of experience. There is nothing wrong with that."[10]

While the actual groundbreaking for construction of the memorial remained on hold due to pending court action, the Supreme Court's 5–4 decision upholding the Florida election favoring George W. Bush meant change at the ABMC. Recognizing that the son of the president who had fired him was not likely going to retain him, General Woerner wrote to the president-elect to request two individuals be retained for continuity purposes—the ABMC secretary, Maj. Gen. John P. Herrling and the chair of the World War II Memorial Committee, Commissioner F. Haydn Williams—arguing that "they both hold critical positions and together they are the directing force behind the building of the national memorial."[11] Simultaneously, the ABMC executive director, Col. Ken Pond, USA (Ret.), wrote a similar letter to the man he anticipated as his new boss—Gen. P. X. Kelley. In his appeal, Pond credited Herrling with eliminating two-thirds of the maintenance backlog at the worldwide cemeteries and monuments under ABMC stewardship, and with overseeing the fundraising campaign that brought in more than $150 million. As for Williams, Pond wrote that the ambassador was unselfish, "repeatedly shuttling from coast to coast, with no personal gain over the past five years." He continued, "As chairman of our World War II Memorial Committee, he personally shepherded the memorial through 21 often contentious public hearings. He is the sole commissioner responsible for the performance of our design team and the invaluable personal rapport established with the approving national commissions. He is also the only Republican commissioner."[12]

Unlike President Clinton, the new President Bush was quicker to appoint a new set of commissioners. Kelley would relieve Woerner as the chairman. Major General Herrling would be retained as secretary. Along with his fellow Clinton-appointed commissioners, Ambassador Williams' term with the ABMC would come to an end. An Italian proverb quoted by Voltaire states, "Perfect is the enemy of good." To that end, Rolly Kidder observed of Williams, "[A]n aspect of his character which sometimes got in the way of getting things done was his own perfectionism. Sometimes, in his attempts to make things more perfect, it could also slow things down." General Woerner opined that the non-reappointment of Williams, the only Republican appointee to the ABMC during the Clinton administration, indicated a frustration with the ambassador's deliberate oversight of the final design process and provided the opportunity to release him. Now that the design was practically complete, that opportunity was taken.[13]

Chapter Ten

ON TO THE DEDICATION

2001–4

THOUGH THE ELECTORAL result had sealed the fate of the Site and Design Committee, most of their work had been completed. Sadly, news reached the SDC that J. Carter Brown had developed some health issues and would not be able to attend future deliberations. Pat Foote wrote a letter to him expressing her dismay about the news and on behalf of the SDC wished Brown and his family a joyful Christmas. Brown wrote back, "I fully hope when this treatment phase is over, I will be back on the barricades with all of you. We have much to accomplish but I have every confidence that all your good work will not have been in vain." Unfortunately for the former head of the National Gallery of Art, he would be diagnosed with multiple myeloma, a terminal blood cancer that would claim his life on June 17, 2002, two years before the dedication of the memorial.[1]

A small consolation for Brown, who had been labeled a leading villain by the memorial's opponents, was that in his dying days he could rest knowing that ground had been broken to build the memorial that he had helped to bring to fruition. Despite the opposition lawsuit filed in October 2000, the well-orchestrated faux groundbreaking ceremony led by the president of the United States seemed to assure the memorial's supporters that, in the end, the courts would rule to allow the project to go forward.

Earlier, the United States District Court had informed the plaintiffs that their October filing could not be heard until a permit to build the memorial was granted. Having demonstrated that the funding was now in place thanks to a phenomenally successful capital campaign, the ABMC had expected a quick turnaround on the application to start construction, but there had been silence from the National Park Service. Given the recent contention, the concern became that opponents of the memorial may have influenced Secretary of the Interior Babbitt to "sit on it." Williams initiated a series of phone calls that reached up to the highest levels in the White House.[2] The Park Service granted that permit on January 23, 2001. Now the legal ballgame began with filing on February 15, to block the GSA from contracting or performing construction on site on behalf of the ABMC. Three weeks later, the opposition also won a ten-day restraining order to prevent the NPS and ABMC from pruning the roots of the elm trees flanking the site.

On April 5, *Boston Globe* critic Robert Campbell would write, "The final battle of World War II is going on in Washington. In the past two weeks it's become so hot it's silly."[3] Campbell then summarized a chain of unforeseen events, starting with a realization that Harvey Gantt of the NCPC had voted on matters pertaining to the World War II Memorial on three occasions after his term had expired. There was nothing nefarious in intent; the reason why Gantt was still sitting in the chairman's chair past his term expiration was that his successor had yet to be appointed. In the past, other chairmen had also hung on to guide the body after term expirations until a new chair could be seated. Indeed, governing rules for the oversight body that traced its origins to 1924 had once sanctioned this practice. However, amended institutional bylaws in 1973, that no one had seemed to have been aware of nearly three decades later, had changed the policy.

For the NCPC, the question was how to mitigate the outcome of those three sessions where Gantt had cast a decisive vote. Gantt's successor, who had to tackle this dilemma, would be a late-term Clinton appointee, Richard Friedman, a Massachusetts-based real estate developer who had built a reputation of converting historic structures into high-end resort properties. Recognizing the dilemma facing one of the governing bodies that had voted to permit the memorial project to go forward, the ABMC announced that no contracts would be let for construction until thirty days following the NCPC's resolution of the three "tainted" votes.[4]

On a flight back to Washington in early March, former Senator Dole expressed his frustration with the pending litigation to Senator Tim Hutchinson. The Arkansas senator subsequently introduced S. 580, a bill that reaffirmed decisions to build the World War II Memorial at the Rainbow Pool site as final, "not to be subject to further administrative or judicial review." Though the bill would be sent to the Committee of Governmental Administration to await further consideration, its introduction led to charges by the opposition and in the media that Congress was intending to subvert the due process mechanisms that had been established by the Constitution. Campbell, the critic who supported the St.Florian design and memorial location, lamented that the Hutchinson bill violated the democratic principles that the World War II veterans had fought for. Campbell cited St.Florian, who concurred that the issue needed to be decided in the courts. In attacking the move by memorial supporters to have the issue resolved once and for all in Congress, Campbell did not leave the opposition off the hook, taking aim at Judy Scott Feldman's assertions that the memorial "was illegally approved by some federal agencies" as blatant lies.[5]

However, there were members of the NCPC who clearly sympathized with Feldman's contentions. On the day Campbell published his column, NCPC chair Friedman issued a written statement that the NCPC intended to host two days of hearing in mid-June "to review its previous actions" on the memorial. Procedures for those June sessions would be determined at the forthcoming May 3 NCPC gathering. In his research for *Their Last Battle*, Nicolaus Mills learned that unlike Gantt, who had been cultivated by Williams, Friedman had issues with the St.Florian design. Thus, the new chairman would be open to reconsidering more than what had been voted on at the three meetings where Gantt should not have been present.[6]

To the great delight of the National Coalition to Save Our Mall and its allies, the NCPC voted to approach the June hearings with an open slate, deciding not only to reconsider votes taken when Gantt had overstayed his tenure as chair but also all previous decisions on the memorial since the commission first approved the Constitution Gardens site in 1995. As for the June meetings, the ABMC and the opposition would be given equal time to state their cases. Impartial experts would be called to testify on the site and design. Top architects and critics who had served as consultants during the competition and later served on sounding board panels need not come. In addition, the NCPC wanted a full-scale mock-up of the memorial to be built.[7]

Whereas Feldman and friends felt upbeat and energized in the wake of the NCPC decisions on the path ahead, those who had worked endless hours to create the plans for the memorial were horrified. Published two days after the NCPC meeting, Benjamin Forgey's column titled "An Overdue Honor for World War II Veterans Once Again is Unjustly in the Line of Fire" captured the sentiments of those favoring the immediate construction of the memorial.[8]

For members of Congress who had endorsed the World War II Memorial, especially those who had attended the faux groundbreaking ceremony six months earlier, the NCPC had steered way out of its lane. The Hutchinson bill sitting with the Committee on Government Affairs morphed into S. 745, a bill drafted by Virginia's Senator John W. Warner, which inserted provisions that could stand up to a court challenge. Though under federal law the ABMC staff were forbidden from lobbying Congress, the commissioners were free to execute their constitutional right and Frank Moore was pressed into service. With many senators and their chiefs of staff still in office two decades after the Carter presidency, Moore's Rolodex proved a valued commodity as Williams and Moore canvassed the upper house to gain support for S. 745. Moore recalled reaching out to at least fifty Senate offices and also visiting the Hill to call on Senators Sam Nunn, Patrick Leahy, Trent Lott, and Richard Shelby. Moore, having ridden back with Congressman Stump on a flight from Phoenix, felt confident that Stump, who had served in the Navy as a pharmacist's mate during World War II, could handle the lower house. On the day the NCPC decided to reconsider the World War II Memorial siting, Congressman Bob Stump from Arizona introduced H.R. 1696, adopting language from Senator Hutchinson's initial legislation. Stump bypassed some committees and spearheaded his bill through two other committees and to a full house vote in twelve days. Moore recalled that when the bill hit the floor for a vote, the congressional World War II veterans, many of whom who were ranking members on the Appropriations and Armed Services committees, all stood up and faced away from the Speaker, facing their junior colleagues with their arms crossed. Stump's bill passed with heavy bipartisan support by a margin of 400–15. A week later on May 22, the House used a voice vote to reapprove H.R. 1696, which now incorporated the more precise language that Warner had used in the Senate version.

The timing of the congressional action coincided with Memorial Day, which allowed the East Room of the White House to serve as a backdrop on the national holiday for the bill signing ceremony with President George W. Bush. The son of a World War II Navy torpedo plane pilot and former president was joined by members of Congress and ABMC commissioners for the occasion.

With President Bush inking his name to Senator Warner's National World War II Memorial Bill, Public Law 107-11 came into effect, enabling the ABMC to proceed with construction. Subsequently, the Justice Department, representing the ABMC, appealed to the U.S. District Court to lift stays imposed to hold up on construction. In response, the attorney representing the opposition filed legal briefs contending that the court still had jurisdiction, because Public

Law 107-11 did not address all of the contentious issues that were being litigated, and questioned the constitutionality of the law, which in essence allowed Congress to eliminate judicial review, violating the separation of powers spelled out in Article III of the Constitution. The briefs failed to achieve their desired goal. On June 7, the court refused to continue the restraining order to halt construction and on August 16, the court dismissed the entire opposition lawsuit, citing the language in Warner's legislation, which made it clear that the agency decisions in this specific case would not be subject to court review. An appeal to the U.S. Court of Appeals that fall failed when, on November 9, a three-judge panel confirmed that Public Law 107-11 had effectively removed court jurisdiction and that Article III had not been violated. Again, the opposition petitioned the U.S. Court of Appeals for the District of Columbia on December 21, 2001. This petition would be turned down six weeks later.[9]

The day the restraining order was lifted, GSA wasted no time in awarding a $56 million contract to the joint venture of Tompkins Builders and Grunley-Walsh Construction Company. Construction work began on August 27, 2001, as contractors fenced off the area around the Rainbow Pool to commence nearly a half year of site preparation. Meanwhile, on July 12, 2001, the White House announced the appointment of the new commissioners for the ABMC. A week earlier, Williams still had hope that he might be reappointed through the lobbying of others. With regards to helping his own cause, the ambassador wrote, "I don't want to lobby for myself and *I won't*—unseemly." Despite the good words put in by others, Williams was not among the list of names released by the White House.

As expected, Gen. P. X. Kelley, USMC (Ret.), would return as the chair. Williams wrote to Kelley to congratulate him. Though they were now former commissioners, Haydn Williams, along with Rolly Kidder, Pat Foote, and Frank Moore, remained committed to supporting the project and formally rebranded themselves as the World War II Memorial Design Consultants, and informally dubbed themselves "the Old Working Group." They met with Friedrich St.Florian on September 30, to review the progress on the inscriptions.

During October, Williams had an amiable breakfast with the new ABMC chairman. General Kelley followed that with a letter to Williams on November 1, thanking him for the breakfast meeting and proposing a meeting with some of the new commissioners. The general promised not to tinker with any of the previously approved design elements but did assert that the new commission intended to review some of the remaining design elements relating to bas reliefs, inscriptions, battle names, and gold stars. Kelley challenged Williams and his now ad hoc group to make recommendations on these issues by the end of the year.[10]

As Williams prepared to mobilize his troops for one last whack at making recommendations for the final unresolved elements, he must have been touched when Major General Herrling presented him with the Distinguished Service Medal, with an accompanying note that stated, "The world will never know what you've done for AMBC but I do." Shortly after receiving this notable award, Williams brought together former commissioners Foote, Kidder, and Moore, along with Helen Fagin and Friedrich St.Florian, for a grueling two-day work session on November 13 and 14. This was to discuss quotes, locations, and other unresolved issues in advance of a site visit by the CFA on November 15, and a meeting with ABMC commissioners scheduled for two weeks later.[11]

Battling cancer, J. Carter Brown mustered enough energy to visit the Rainbow Pool site along with a delegation of his commissioners. Much had changed for the nation as well as at the site in the year since the faux groundbreaking ceremony. The terrorist attacks on the World Trade Center and Pentagon on September 11 had taken a greater toll of human life than the Japanese attack on Pearl Harbor, and the media was quick to draw parallels with the recent attacks and that earlier "Day of Infamy." The nation was again at war, and at least for now, unified in a way that the new memorial was intended to symbolize. At the fenced-in site, the sidewalks around the Rainbow Pool had been peeled away and the area now resembled a mud pit. During excavation, workers were surprised to discover the foundation of a World War I–era Navy structure, undocumented electrical lines, and that the storm-water drainage pipes from the former Rainbow Pool leading to the Tidal Basin were cracked, exposing groundwater in the vicinity to potential pollutants.[12]

Emerging out of his portable manager's hut, Barry Owenby greeted Brown and turned to the design team of Williams, St.Florian, and Ray Kaskey to brief the visitors on design elements that had been resolved or that needed resolution. Kaskey took pride in showing off the final flagpole design and a more detailed model of sculptured eagles that were to be placed at the 17th Street entrances. Kaskey showed Brown and his colleagues some adjustments that had been made to the ropes in the balustrades and a change in the material that would back the field of stars. St.Florian presented his plans, which had been suggested by the NPS, to introduce low museum-style benches on the west side of the new Rainbow Pool. Brown pushed back against the idea as they took away from open space. Williams offered a compromise of installing benches at a later date after the memorial opening, should they be deemed necessary. Brown and his fellow commissioners were asked to comment on six styles of font for the inscriptions.[13]

On November 30, Williams reassembled his team, minus St.Florian, at the Leo A. Daly conference room, where they met with General Kelley and three of the other newly appointed commissioners, Gen. Frederick M. Franks, Lt. Gen. Julius W. Becton, and historian/biographer Joseph E. Persico. During the morning session the group reviewed the wording selected for placement at nineteen locations. For the afternoon, Kaskey and St.Florian joined in for the discussion on remaining design elements. Likewise, the group readdressed the backdrop material for the gold stars and agreed that over time, bronze would serve the purpose more effectively than granite.[14]

Regarding the inscriptions, given her maternal role serving to inspire others during the Great Depression and World War II, it seemed logical that a quote from Eleanor Roosevelt would adorn the memorial at some location. However, two weeks after the end of the November summit, an exasperated Williams faxed a memorandum to Fagin—Subject: "Quotes from Eleanor Roosevelt"—where he lamented, "Unfortunately I had great difficulty in finding

Mrs. Roosevelt statements which would sound 'poetic' or even uplifting." The ambassador sent fifteen samples to illustrate his quandary. Undeterred, Fagin traveled to Hyde Park to visit the FDR Library and successfully extracted several chisel-worthy quotes from the former first lady.[15]

Had Williams had his way, Roosevelt's quote would have been one of dozens adorning every available open space of granite. However, St.Florian, with the strong backing of Brown, convinced Williams for the need to leave some open space to prevent reader fatigue and to make the quotes selected even more impactful.[16]

With that, Williams finalized the end-of-year Design Consultants report with final recommendations to General Kelley and submitted it on December 31. Subsequently, at hearings held on March 21 by the Commission of Fine Arts and on April 4 by the National Capital Planning Commission, those recommendations pertaining to the flagpoles and gold star backdrops were formally approved. However, the issue of inscriptions came to the fore when word got back to Williams that some of the new ABMC commissioners saw an opportunity to make a lasting "literal" imprint by substituting their preferences. The secretary, Maj. Gen. Herrling, sent the Old Working Group a broader list of quotations being considered. Helen Fagin wrote back to Herrling, "As a member of ABMC's original World War II Memorial Committee representing the Museum Advisory Board, it is indeed very rewarding to me to know, and I'm sure to my colleagues of the former World War II Memorial Committee, that after many long discussions and considerations of hundreds of different alternatives in terms of themes, text, and locations, our choices are being given careful scrutiny by members of your new World War II Memorial Committee."

Fagin further winced at a proposed alteration of an Archibald MacLeish line from a poem the former Librarian of Congress had written after the war, which had read, "OUR DEATHS ARE NOT OURS, THEY ARE YOURS, THEY WILL MEAN WHAT YOU MAKE OF THEM." The new proposed words read, "WE LEAVE YOU OUR DEATHS, GIVE THEM MEANING." In the end the inscription drafted by Joe Persico benignly read, "HERE WE MARK THE PRICE OF FREEDOM."[17]

The inscription alterations tried Williams' patience. There was some discussion within the Old Working Group to approach the CFA at their next hearing and challenge the new ABMC-proposed inscriptions. However, Fagin wrote to Williams cautioning against a strategy that might be seen as sour grapes and only increase the perception of a growing rift between the incumbents and their predecessors. Instead, she suggested that Williams simply attend the next CFA meeting to give a personal tribute to the now gravely ill chairman J. Carter Brown. However, before he could do so Brown died. Williams would serve as one of the deceased chairman's honorary pallbearers.[18] For one inscription, the Old Working Group did push back and prevailed. Foote, reviewing the great white men of history statements that the successor male commissioners had chosen for chiseling into the granite, noted that a quote attributed to Eleanor Roosevelt and another to a Women's Army Corps major had been scratched by the new commissioners. Foote wrote to General Kelley to express her dismay and remind him that some 400,000 women had served in the armed forces during the war. Receiving no response after thirty days, Foote sent a second letter. There was still no response at the time of MAB member Sarah McClendon's passing on January 8, 2003. Attending the memorial service at the National Press Club, Foote sat with Helen Thomas. Foote shared with Thomas her frustration over the quote deletions. Thomas asked Foote to send her copies of the letters she had sent to Kelley and additional background material on the quotation selection process. Thomas would subsequently publish a column railing against the elimination of women's quotations. Shortly thereafter, Foote was assured that a quote from Col. Oveta Culp Hobby would be included. Today visitors to the memorial can read "WOMEN WHO STEPPED UP WERE MEASURED AS CITIZENS OF THE NATION, NOT AS WOMEN. THIS WAS A PEOPLE'S WAR AND EVERYONE WAS IN IT."[19]

As the ABMC approached the first anniversary of the actual beginning of construction, General Kelley took pleasure in reporting to the former commissioners and members of the MAB that site preparations were ahead of schedule, making note of the pouring of the slurry wall. One of the hidden aspects of the memorial is that it sits within a two-foot-thick concrete bathtub that was created by digging a trench down to bedrock, in this case thirty-five to forty-five feet below street level. As the dirt was excavated, a "slurry" mixture of bentonite clay and water filled the deepening trench to prevent collapse. With the dirt removed, tubes pushed concrete down to the bedrock depths and the heavier material displaced the soupy mixture, which was extracted and hauled away. The hardened wall now protected the future structure from surges in groundwater tables, which could undermine the foundations. To provide additional support, nearly six hundred steel piles would be driven down into the bedrock. In contrast, to the surprise of all, when the original Rainbow Pool was peeled away, the anticipated log piling supports were nonexistent. In addition to reporting site construction progress, Kelley also reported that the CFA had approved of the Kaskey-designed bas reliefs. Given the limitations on using inscriptions to tell the narrative of the war, the bas reliefs would carry the load of the storytelling element. The bronze panels, each five feet, four inches long and one foot, ten inches high, would depict the transformation of the country during the war in the Pacific and Atlantic theaters. Flanking the memorial plaza entrance area on 17th Street, the twelve panels on the south side told the narrative of the war against Japan while the twelve panels on the north side covered the efforts to defeat Italy and then Germany.[20]

For Williams and his fellow members of the former SDC, there was little more to do except to receive progress reports of the construction. On Veterans Day 2002, two years after the faux groundbreaking ceremony, General Kelley announced that the World War II Memorial would be dedicated on Saturday, May 29, 2004, beginning with a morning service at the National Cathedral. Four days of festivities on the National Mall would continue as the sixtieth anniversary of D-Day approached. Kelley was also pleased to announce that the capital campaign's fundraising to support the construction had reached $189 million. A few months earlier, Williams had received a letter from MAB chairman Peter Wheeler stating, "I remember at the very beginning we made a national study that indicated we would only be able to raise $40 million. You were wise enough to look into the future and, in a very diplomatic way, explain that we needed to set $100 million as our goal."[21]

As the designer of the memorial, St.Florian commuted to Washington to witness the creation of the collective vision. At first his visits were infrequent during the excavation and pile-driving phase. Once the mechanical facilities were covered over, St.Florian found himself in Washington on at least a monthly basis. Arriving at the ABMC-GSA trailer, he would be greeted by the on-site project executive Barry Owenby. However, St.Florian fended off Owenby and others who offered to accompany him around the site, so he could focus on aspects of the construction. Watching St.Florian through a pair of binoculars as he wandered around the yard, Owenby made notes of where the designer stopped and closely studied something. In addition to coming to Washington, St.Florian went to the quarry in Vermont to witness the trial Memorial Arch assembly, fearing that the supports would not be able to handle the weight. Writing to Williams in mid-2003, the architect wrote how he wished Williams could personally witness the fruits of their joint labor come together: "I know now with great certainty that the memorial will redeem itself beyond our expectations."[22]

At the time of St.Florian's note, much of the stonework had been put in place, with work commencing on the stone balconies beginning back in February. The below-surface pump rooms had been completed and roofed over. Stone carvers began their inscription work. To find the skilled craftsmen to perform this work, St.Florian looked down Narragansett Bay to the John Stevens Shop, the nation's oldest family business. A stone-engraving business that had operated from the same Newport workshop since 1705, the company's eleven-generation reputation was being upheld by Nicholas Benson, who designed a unique "Roman Claudian Variant" font for the eighteen inscriptions that would be placed at twenty locations. (Two sets of inscriptions would be repeated at the flagpole benches and within the two arches.)[23]

During the home stretch of the project, much of the focus concentrated on what has been claimed as "the largest bronze project in contemporary history." Ray Kaskey's Brentwood studio produced the two baldachinos for the north and south archways, which together were composed of eight columns, eight eagles, and the two large wreaths that would be suspended from the eagles' beaks. Each of the eight eagles weighed 20,000 pounds. The two bronze wreaths each weighed 8,000 pounds. Stainless steel ribbons, suspended from the beak of each eagle, were designed to suspend the wreath within each archway.

To produce the twenty-four bas reliefs, Kaskey worked with World War II reenactors and era photography to create the three-dimensional displays. Each panel depicted at least eight figures, and more than one hundred hours were required to shape the clay into place for each panel. The members of the Old Working Group looked over the panels to conduct a final reality check. Frank Moore recalled looking at a jeep being hooked up to be lifted onto a ship. Something wasn't right. Then it occurred to him that the jeep's upright windshield would have been folded down and secured onto the hood. The change was made. Likewise, Pat Foote made sure the models reflected proper female hair length and even recommended changes on the heels of the women's footwear. The clay panels were then shipped to Chester, Pennsylvania, home of the Laran Foundry, which had a reputation as one of the world's premier art casting facilities. At first, liquefied rubber was poured over the clay model and, once hardened, peeled off to create a mold that was filled with hot wax. The wax version of the clay model was next pressed down into a sand-like ceramic slurry. When the ceramic hardened, the wax could be melted away, leaving a mold that could now withstand the pouring of liquid bronze. Kaskey and his artisans would also create 1,048 sculpted gold stars for the Freedom Wall, 112 bronze wreaths with armatures, an interior and exterior wreath for each pillar, and 52 bronze rope castings to connect those pillars. Finally, Kaskey had responsibility for the creation of the two enormous flagpoles that would front 17th Street.[24]

With the gold stars installed on the Freedom Wall in early 2004, St.Florian opened his copy of the *Providence Journal* one morning in early February to see a picture of the creation. Subsequently he wrote to Williams, recalling the first time the ambassador had seen the design on paper, "I will never forget when you sat silently in front of the first print of the stars in Leo A. Daly's conference room." On March 1, Williams finally traveled to Washington when Major General Herrling brought the Old Working Group together for a preview visit to the new memorial. With Barry Owenby serving as the guide through the near-completed structure, the members of the group donned hard hats and inspected the archways, the pillars, the Freedom Wall, the inscriptions, the bas reliefs, and the dozens of other minute details that they had toiled over. They came away impressed with the quality of the construction and that the project had come in ahead of schedule and under budget. At the end of the tour, the group stood at the Freedom Wall for a victory pose as Williams led the group in doffing their hard hats in a celebratory gesture.[25]

A month ahead of the formal dedication on April 29, the fences came down and the general public had their first opportunity to walk onto the granite plaza and peer up into the archways of Washington's newest landmark. The next day, Herrling wrote to Williams on what it was like to be on the Mall on that bright sunny spring day as he strolled around the site with Owenby, marveling at the crowds and the relaxed atmosphere surrounding the occasion. Citing the *Washington Post*, he further wrote, "Thousands of people—busloads of students, cane-toting veterans escorted by their grown-up children, office workers on their lunch break—got their first glimpse of a memorial that had been 17 years in the making." Herrling concluded, "Bottom line: The World War II Memorial is something special."[26]

EPILOGUE

Wither the pending dedication of the World War II Memorial, an estimated 315,000 citizens arrived in the nation's capital for what was billed as the largest reunion ever to be staged for those who had served in this conflict. Dubbed "A Tribute to a Generation," the salute to those who served, not only overseas but also on the home front, had several components. Beginning on May 27, 2003, the Smithsonian Institution's Center for Folklife and Cultural Heritage, in partnership with ABMC and numerous other institutions, welcomed the public to the four-day National World War II Reunion. Under sunny skies, the veterans, the youngest of whom were in their late seventies, basked in the warm weather as they worked their way through a series of tents placed along the Mall east of the Washington Monument, in the vicinity of the Smithsonian Castle. Among the attractions were two large music pavilions that hosted the Big Band sounds and music of Glenn Miller, Tommy and Jimmy Dorsey, Louis Armstrong, and the Andrews Sisters. The recently established Library of Congress Veterans History Project hosted on-stage interviews with celebrities who had served in the war and set up kiosks to capture the stories of those who had gone on to have productive lives with less notoriety. The National Archives facilitated workshops on how to preserve photographs, artifacts, and written records and organize scrap books. The Veterans Administration and Defense Department also set up information booths to highlight benefit programs and

153

resources. There even was a pavilion that featured an exhibit on the planning and building of the World War II Memorial![1]

For those veterans who were inclined to sit and be serenaded by military ensembles, the "Salute to World War II Veterans" program featured the top instrumental and vocal performers from ceremonial and musical units stationed around the capital. Four two-hour performances held at the MCI Center featured Army, Navy, Marine Corps, Air Force, and Coast Guard performers.

The actual dedication of the memorial provided the climax on the third of the four days, Saturday, May 29. That morning, tens of thousands of people began filling chairs that had been placed to the east of the new memorial, reaching up toward the base of the Washington Monument. Some 117,000 tickets had been distributed, with an estimated 60 percent of the requesters being veterans. More than 30,000 more arrived to observe events, and video screens were set up along the periphery. Ironically, the staging and tents placed on 17th Street to accommodate all of the VIPs practically blotted out the new memorial from the line of sight of the tens of thousands in attendance. As veterans, their families, and friends made their way to their perches, in the northwestern section of the capital a preliminary ceremony commenced at the National Cathedral. The enormous Gothic structure hosted an interfaith service that began at 10 a.m. Featured speakers included the former chairman of the Joint Chiefs, Gen. John W. Vessey, USA (Ret.); the former commandant of the Marine Corps and ABMC chairman Gen. P. X. Kelley; and former President George H. W. Bush. Helen Fagin, seated near the front because she was still in an official capacity as a member of the Memorial Advisory Board, recalled a memorable service where vocal renditions from the war years were interspersed among the numerous patriotic speeches. "I even remember how impressed I was by the chiming of the bells as we were leaving the Cathedral."[2]

As Fagin and others were loaded onto buses that would transport them to the Mall for the official dedication ceremony at 2 p.m., pre-ceremony festivities included musical ensembles, video recordings of combat in the Atlantic and Pacific, and the unveiling of a new stamp by the postmaster general showing the new memorial. Congresswoman Marcy Kaptur took the opportunity to welcome the veterans. As she did in the groundbreaking ceremony, Kaptur acknowledged the pivotal role played by one of her constituents and acknowledged the support of her fellow legislators in getting the legislation through, especially the World War II veterans in the House and Senate. She then introduced a video showing the construction of the new landmark.

When those who had attended the morning service at the National Cathedral had arrived and filed into the front rows of seats, the official dedication commenced at 2 p.m. with a presentation of state flags and an invocation by a former World War II chaplain, Archbishop Philip M. Hannan. To the left and right of the podium, those assigned to the premier seating sections associated with the project stood and bowed their heads. Haydn Williams stood among this group of current ABMC commissioners, members of the MAB, and other prominent dignitaries. Other former commissioners such as Rolly Kidder were seated in the VIP sections immediately below the stage. As he had done earlier at the cathedral, the ABMC chair General Kelley welcomed all in attendance to the dedication of a memorial to mark the service and sacrifices made during what he labeled as "the most significant event in the history of mankind." The former commandant turned the podium over to a quartet of notable speakers including national news anchor Tom Brokaw, actor Tom Hanks, and national campaign cochairs Senator Robert Dole and Frederick W. Smith. President George W. Bush, flanked by his immediate predecessor, President Clinton, and by his father George Herbert Walker Bush, looked on at the speakers and at the reactions of the crowd from their seats off to the side of the podium. As a reminder of the memorial's symbolism of national unity, nearby sat Senator John Kerry, the presumptive Democratic nominee to challenge the incumbent Bush that fall. Also present was eighty-three-year-old Joseph Lesniewski, who had served with Easy Company of the 101st Airborne Division and had been profiled by Stephen Ambrose in *Band of Brothers*.

The *New York Times* reported that the eighty-year-old Dole "provided the emotional high point of the program" when he exclaimed, "What we dedicate today is not a memorial to war. Rather, it is a tribute to the physical and moral courage that makes heroes out of farm and city boys and that inspired Americans in every generation to lay down their lives for people they will never meet, for ideals that make life itself worth living."

Then, quiet prevailed as the sound of a lone Marine bugle resonated from within the new outdoor structure. The tens of thousands in attendance discerned the familiar melody of "Taps." Once the bugler completed his solemn chore, General Kelley presented the memorial to President George W. Bush. The son of the former commander in chief took to the podium to address one of the largest gatherings of his presidency. The junior Bush accepted the memorial on behalf of the American people and noted that St. Florian's structure was "a fitting tribute, open and expansive, like America; grand and enduring, like the achievements we honor." The president continued, "At this place, at this memorial, we acknowledge a debt of long standing to an entire generation of Americans—those who died, those who fought and worked and grieved and went on. They saved our country and thereby saved the liberty of mankind. And now I ask every man and woman who saw and lived World War II, every member of that generation, to please rise as you are able and receive the thanks of our great nation." With that, veterans from all fifty states rose in unison, many overcoming the frailties of age, to stand, most wearing either ballcaps or garrison caps festooned with pins or ribbons, many others donning their old uniforms, showing pride in their service.

Following the president's address, Denyce Graves led the singing of "The Star-Spangled Banner" and "God Bless America." Barry C. Black, the former Navy chief of chaplains and chaplain of the U.S. Senate, offered the closing benediction.[3]

For a large percentage in the audience, the dedication had been cathartic, as television coverage panned to numerous veterans who had difficulty fighting off the tears. Speaking with a *New York Times* reporter, seventy-eight-year-old

Gale Cornwell of Kingman, Arizona, wept, observing, "So many old friends who aren't here, they're all gone now."

For Williams, Fagin, Kidder, Moore, Foote, and the others who had worked so hard to bring the concept of a memorial to reality, there was deep gratification in seeing the masses of appreciative veterans who had just been acknowledged by their nation for their service during the greatest war of the twentieth century. That evening, Williams hosted the former SDC, along with Friedrich St.Florian and key members of his design team, for a celebratory dinner at the Cosmos Club. Afterward, they made their way back down to the Mall to stand in awe of the edifice that they had created, lit up under the darkening skies. Fagin remembered meeting one veteran in a wheelchair who introduced himself as one of the "battling bastards of Bataan."[4]

In the aftermath of the four-day "Tribute to a Generation" capped by the dedication ceremony, hundreds of thousands more tourists and veterans visited the Mall that summer with the intent to view the newest memorial in the nation's capital. In San Francisco, Williams received a nice letter from ABMC executive director, Kenneth Pond, who exclaimed that "the long-awaited dedication of the National World War II Memorial in May was a tremendous success" and attached an ABMC certificate of appreciation! As for the responsibility for maintaining the new memorial, in November the ABMC turned the site over to the NPS.

The members of the Old Working Group kept in close contact. Having thought more on the idea of writing a book to document their experience, they gathered and organized documents, produced chapter outlines, and interviewed some of the participants in the process. Williams wrote to David Childs about the book-by-committee project to seek some potential introductory remarks. Childs, who had won the competition to design the replacement skyscraper—Freedom Tower—to replace the Twin Towers destroyed on 9/11, wrote back offering his best wishes and support for the narrative. Unfortunately, some of the momentum for the project lost steam as Williams remained on the West Coast tending to Margaret, who now suffered from

Parkinson's disease. She passed away on Thanksgiving Day 2005 at the Redwoods, an assisted living facility located across the Golden Gate in Mill Valley. Having turned eighty-six, Williams had his own health issues to contend with.[5]

During the fall of 2006, Pat Foote visited the memorial to evaluate how it had fared under the stewardship of the NPS, and she submitted a memorandum for the record to her former SDC colleagues. She observed that some of the elm trees along the periphery had been lost, and that many of the perennials planted back in 2004 had not endured. Foote observed that the Garden of Remembrance, placed to the northwest of the plaza, seemed unkempt and was not being used as a contemplative area for families to reflect. Meeting with Vikki Keys of the NPS, Foote also learned of some of the mechanical and lighting issues—several of the fountains leaked within the mechanical room and eighty-eight small lights were not working.[6]

The memorandum served as an advance scouting report for a reconvening of three members of the Old Working Group as Williams, Kidder, and Foote arrived in Washington at the end of October. Williams flew in from San Francisco with an agenda broader than addressing the issue of dying plants and leaky fountains. On Monday, October 30, the now eighty-seven-year-old Williams began the day by presiding over a working breakfast at the Cosmos Club. The ambassador laid out his primary objectives of seeing if the NPS would consider a separate contract for landscape maintenance and cleaning, and if the ABMC would be willing to fund that from the $14 million surplus that was being maintained in a trust fund. The group then reviewed the most recent ABMC annual report to note that the actual cost of building the memorial had come to $133 million, with an additional $36.5 million expended to support the fundraising campaign. Williams opined that perhaps the ABMC could annually release $500,000 from the trust to support memorial upkeep in a way comparable to its overseas memorials and cemeteries. In addition, Williams floated a thought about setting up a nonprofit organization to provide additional means of support, which he would fund through a bequest in his will. Foote latched onto the idea of a "Friends of the World War II

Memorial" and envisioned a board that would meet twice a year, made up of ex officio members of the National Park Service, Department of Defense, and Veterans Administration, as well as military historians. Closing out their breakfast session, they again broached the subject of documenting the history of building the memorial, with Foote suggesting that someone ought to sit with Williams to conduct an oral history. Kidder stepped in to remind all that "Haydn doesn't talk the way he writes." Williams agreed with this observation.

From the Cosmos Club, the small entourage made their way to the memorial to view some of the maintenance issues. Following lunch, the Old Working Group met at the office of Jim van Sweden, joined by Friedrich St.Florian, Ray Kaskey, Barry Owenby, Sheila Brady, and the host, van Sweden. St.Florian made some recommendations on proposals to widen the sidewalks along the exterior of the embracing arms, and noted that the lithochrome process used to make the inscriptions stand out was failing due to weathering. Kaskey happily reported that there were no bird problems within the baldachinos; however, wasp nests had become an issue. The sculptor also noted that rust spots had appeared on some of the stars. Suspecting the corrosive effects of fireworks, Kaskey recommended that the Wall of Freedom be covered during the annual Fourth of July display. Owenby, speaking on behalf of the ABMC, noted that, of the funds remaining in the trust, $900,000 had been allocated for the sidewalk widening project mentioned by St.Florian and another half million was being set aside for security cameras. Regarding the lighting, Owenby recommended simply removing numerous fixtures as a form of addition by subtraction. He also opined that the Garden of Remembrance had been located too far from the main plaza to serve its intended purpose. Owenby lamented that the NPS had not been properly maintaining the memorial and he saw no improvement pending, exclaiming, "If they could at least maintain it to 50 percent of ABMC standards maybe I can accept it—but they don't." With regards to Williams' idea of tapping the trust to support maintenance, Owenby argued that laws prohibited such interagency transfers of funding.

That evening the group returned to the Cosmos Club to have a working dinner with the new secretary of the ABMC, Brig. Gen. John W. Nicholson, in attendance. President Bush had nominated Nicholson to replace Herrling in January 2005 following the turnover of the memorial to the NPS. Nicholson took notes as the Old Working Group discussed the day's events. After his departure following a successful tenure as the ABMC secretary, Major General Herrling was invited to lead an even more daunting fundraising challenge—a National Museum for the United States Army to be located at Fort Belvoir in northern Virginia.

The next morning featured yet another Cosmos Club working breakfast, this time with the aforementioned Herrling in attendance. The group then proceeded to van Sweden's office for late-morning briefings from Vikki Keys of the NPS, who held responsibility for the core Mall memorials. Keys noted that the NPS had volunteers to augment the four park rangers assigned to interpret the memorial and floated the idea of a trust for the Mall to support all of the memorials. Keys admitted that maintenance funding was wholly inadequate for all of the memorials and monuments under her charge. Meeting again with Nicholson and the staff at ABMC, Williams and his colleagues came away frustrated that no funds from the trust could be applied to support ongoing maintenance.[7]

In the wake of the meetings held at the end of October 2006, the Old Working Group continued to correspond. Following a meeting in February 2007 between Ambassador Williams and Congresswoman Kaptur, Williams convened a meeting of the group, hosted by Frank Moore, to draft bylaws for a nonprofit organization. Subsequently, on March 27, 2007, Williams drafted "Friends of the National World War II Memorial Inc. Memo # 1" with a stated purpose "of helping the World War II Memorial become all we hoped it would be." Eventually that mission statement would morph into "honoring and preserving the national memory of World War II and to creating the next 'Greatest Generation' of tomorrow." As with his role as chair of the World War II Memorial Committee, Williams continued to prove his worth as the leader of the new nonprofit organization, recruiting not only individuals who had a role in building the memorial, but also seeking those who could champion the new organization's mission over the long term. He continued as a taskmaster with an eye toward getting involved with the nitty-gritty. For example, he championed the "Friends" logo incorporating the rope symbolizing unity across the base. He also recognized that volunteers would be vital to provide interpretation of the symbolic elements, the inscriptions, and the bas reliefs, and reviewed volunteer cue cards to ensure factual correctness.

Williams served as the chairman of the Friends for two years, stepping down when he reached the age of ninety. However, he remained active with the group as chairman emeritus, as the organization took on sponsorship of an annual public lecture series featuring prominent historians; began hosting an annual teachers' conference in Washington, D.C., about the significance of the conflict; and started collecting and archiving video interviews of World War II veterans and those who served on the home front as surviving members of the Greatest Generation entered their twilight years. In addition, the Friends of the National World War II Memorial has assumed the lead responsibility in planning, staging, and funding five or more major national commemorative events annually.

The ambassador lived on to see the tenth anniversary of his beloved memorial. Returning to Washington, he participated in a 2014 Memorial Day ceremony at the memorial, an entity that the park service now estimated 4 million visitors saw annually. Sitting next to Williams while listening to Senator Dole addressing the gathered audience, Helen Fagin clutched the ambassador's hand and told Williams that he ought to be the one addressing the crowd. Instead, Williams drafted a statement for the Friends of the National World War II Memorial website, reflecting on the growing popularity of the site, referring to it in a way as "Washington's village square, the town green on the Mall, a place for silent solemn remembrance, a place to linger, to stroll, to talk, to listen, to share memory and meaning."

What impressed Williams was the number of school groups visiting the memorial, and how the memorial accommodated concerts performed by various high school bands and other youth ensembles. He noted how the Friends had developed a teachers' outreach program and lesson plans to teach the history of the conflict. As for the veterans, the memorial had become a mecca: "There they see 'their' memorial. In person, they sense its presence and meaning, they reminisce, revel in the company of fellow G.Is, and are made to feel remembered, saluted, and honored. These highly emotional, moving, heart-lifting occasions at the Memorial give life and meaning to the words 'a grateful nation remembers.'"

Williams spoke to the memorial itself and the important symbolism of national unity. Speaking of the 4,048 Gold Stars, each representing approximately one hundred fallen service personnel, Williams observed, "If these silent stars could speak, Archibald MacLeish would have them say, 'We leave you our deaths, give them their meaning.'" Clearly the ambassador desired to leave a lasting reminder that the current inscription over the stars was not of his choosing.[8]

With the memorial serving as a reunion site for those who had fought in the conflict, it also had served as a reunion site for those who had fought to get it built. Following the tenth anniversary event at the memorial, Williams hosted what proved to be a final reunion luncheon for those involved in the siting, designing, and building of the memorial. Rolly Kidder tried to save the ambassador a few dollars by substituting chicken for crab cake. Williams would have none of it! Following a sumptuous celebratory luncheon, several of the key actors took turns to reflect on what had been accomplished. Congresswoman Kaptur took great pride in the project that she initiated and the tremendous support it received along the way. Kidder reflected on the search for a site and how Williams, standing at the Rainbow Pool, had recognized that "[t]his is where it needs to be." St.Florian spoke about "the client," observing that Williams was at times his harshest critic but became a fine mentor. As a designer, he felt that, thanks to the site, he had been given a gift that could harness the power of both Washington and Lincoln. As an immigrant, St.Florian appreciated what it meant to be free, and the memorial stood for that. Another immigrant, Helen Fagin, echoed St.Florian's comments, saying that she had been given a gift to work on the eleven-year endeavor and observed that only in America could a Holocaust survivor be invited to the White House to work on such a project. Fagin was acknowledged for her arguments to incorporate the ropes in the design to show the strength of the country. Major General Herrling was there to remind attendees that there had been some serious battles but in the end they came together. Harry Robinson, representing the CFA as J. Carter Brown's successor, spoke of this project as Carter's opus, reminding everyone that Carter's father had been assigned during the war to recover stolen works of art. John Parsons, formerly of the NPS, recounted the debate between the approval authorities on site selection and the importance of that August 1995 conference call. Ray Kaskey thanked St.Florian for the opportunity to work on this project, and St.Florian spoke of the synergetic effort between the two. The sculptor took great pride in his eagles, each draping ribbons to support a wreath. He said the structural engineers had claimed this was not feasible. Kaskey proved them wrong. Finally, Pat Foote had an opportunity to address the group, noting that Williams did get upset with some of the opposition's tactics and she took pride in her aggressive defense of the memorial project, especially in the moniker "That Horrible Woman."

After celebratory toasts, that evening the group drove down to the memorial with Williams and his caregiver, who traveled with him. With a wheelchair broken open, the "Father of the World War II Memorial" was rolled down to the plaza. The Navy World War II veteran looked out at the fountains and the Wall of Freedom and took in the surroundings as the skies darkened and the lighting transformed the complex. The next day he would leave for San Francisco, never to return.

"It is with great sadness that the Friends of the National World War II Memorial announces today that its founder and chairman emeritus, F. Haydn Williams, has died at the age of 96 in San Francisco, California." Posted on April 22, 2016, the day of his passing, the online tribute spoke of Williams as the "Father" of the National World War II Memorial as well as the founder of the Friends organization.

Two weeks later, the Friends of the National World War II Memorial again convened for a celebration of life ceremony and wreath-laying at the memorial, and then again at a luncheon held in Williams' honor. With Rolly Kidder serving as the master of ceremony for both events, several of the principals—including St.Florian, Kaskey, Herrling, Owenby, and Parsons—shared their emotional farewells. However, perhaps the most eloquent statement came from Florida. Judith Fagin read the words of her mother, which captured the sentiments of all who had worked with Williams:

> What a painful thought—to have to offer parting last words for our beloved Haydn.
>
> Well. These may be my parting last words—but never my parting thoughts!
>
> Haydn's dignified presence, his vivid image, his quiet yet authoritative voice and a unique manner of speech and persuasion, his always friendly smile, and his old-fashioned correspondence by handwriting in black pen on a yellow pad—all of these personal attributes are etched in one's memory forever. They are exclusively Haydn's.
>
> But more—much, much more than that—to us who knew him and worked with him, it was F. Haydn Williams *the man*—the paradigm of impeccable personal and professional integrity, the ultimate American Patriot, the reliable FRIEND.
>
> To those who may not know it—Ambassador Haydn Williams was no easy taskmaster—when he took over the leadership of the WWII Memorial's Site and Design Committee, his commitment was serious and determined to memorialize and fully honor the World War II American Soldiers with [the] highest dignity— and no one gave this task more effort, more time, more selfless commitment.

My proudest memories of working with Haydn and the Site and Design Committee, as "a fellow worker in a great and noble cause" (his words engraved on a silver platter he presented to the World War II Memorial "Working Group"), will always remain his sometimes stubborn but always enlightening and instructive leadership at the tough decision-making weekend meetings. He always gave us assignments and expected the research/work [to be] done by the next meeting—no questions asked. It was hard and demanding work—but so very exhilarating and so rewarding! We simply formed an extended family—and remained close friends to this very sad moment, together deeply mourning our Beloved Leader.

Haydn's favored inscription for the Sacred Precinct of the WWII Memorial memorializing heroes would have been a quotation from Archibald MacLeish's poem, asking for recognition of their sacrifice, "We leave you our deaths, give them their meaning."

It is indeed Ambassador F. Haydn Williams, a distinguished WWII Veteran and American hero, who became this country's fitting arbiter in the fulfillment of this eternal legacy.

How proud he made us to be Americans!!!

Thank you, Haydn, for the gift of knowing you—I shall remember you always in my heart and in my soul.[9]

NOTES

Preface

1. Friedrich St.Florian, interview with author, June 26, 2019.
2. Christopher Shea, "The Brawl on the Mall," *Preservation*, January/February 2001, 40.
3. Kirk Savage, *Monument Wars: Washington, D.C., the National Mall, and the Transformation of the Washington Landscape* (Berkeley and Los Angeles: University of California Press, 2009); Shea, "The Brawl on the Mall," 40.
4. Savage, *Monument Wars*, 245; Nicolaus Mills, *Their Last Battle: The Fight for the National World War II Memorial* (New York: Basic Books, 2004), 1–2.
5. Mills, *Their Last Battle*, 9–13.
6. Mills, 12–14.

Chapter 1. Enter F. Haydn Williams

1. Admiral Crowe Biography file, Navy Department Library, Naval History and Heritage Command (NHHC); *Oral History of Admiral William J. Crowe, Jr. U.S. Navy (Retired)*, interview by Paul Stillwell (Washington, D.C.: Naval Historical Foundation, 2009), 5–6, 465–69.
2. Crowe, *Oral History*, 690, 695.
3. Rolly Kidder, narrative provided to author.
4. Crowe, *Oral History*, 697.
5. Naval Reserve Officers Register (1944), Navy Department Library. Williams DD-214 released by the National Military Records Center.
6. VR-12 Command Histories, AR/180, Box V 12–24, Naval History and Heritage Command.

7. Williams subsequently passed the bugle on to Rolly Kidder.

8. "F. Haydn Williams Named Deputy Assistant Secretary of Defense," Department of Defense News Release No. 1074–58, October 27, 1958; *Political Science Review* 51 (Sept. 1957): 800; the Asia Foundation website, https://asiafoundation.org.

9. Margaret F. Williams obituary in the *San Francisco Chronicle*, December 2, 2005; Shirley Baldwin, phone interview with author, February 15, 2019.

10. *The Asia Foundation: Past, Present, and Future*, https://archive.org/details /AsiaFoundationPastPresentAndFuture.

11. *The Asia Foundation: Past, Present, and Future*; See: Henry Luce Foundation Fellowships, https://www.hluce.org/fellowships/; Jan Evans Houser, phone interview with author, March 2, 2019.

12. Margaret Williams obituary.

13. F. Haydn Williams, interviewed by Howard P. Willens and Deanne C. Siemer, February 2, 1999.

14. Crowe, *Oral History*, 698.

15. Crowe, 710–11.

16. Crowe, 714.

17. Memorandum for the President from Henry A. Kissinger, Subject "Micronesia: Final Stages of Negotiations with the Northern Marianas," dated February 6, 1975.

18. See: American Memorial Park, Northern Mariana Islands, https://www.nps.gov /amme/index.htm.

19. See: Saipan Memorial, https://www.abmc.gov/cemeteries-memorials/pacific /saipan-memorial. According to Rolland Kidder, Margaret and Haydn Williams provided most of the funding for the Carillon Bell Tower.

20. Rear Admiral Bitoff and Vice Admiral Baldwin, e-mails to author, February 16, 2019.

21. General Woerner, phone interview with author, February 28, 2019.

22. William J. Crowe Jr. with David Chanoff, *In the Line of Fire* (New York: Simon & Schuster, 1993), 339.

23. "21 Military Leaders Endorse Bill Clinton for President," Clinton Campaign press release dated October 12, 1994. General Woerner, phone interview with author, June 11, 2019.

24. Woerner interview, February 28, 2019.

25. See: American Battle Monuments Commission, https://www.abmc.gov/.

26. See: U.S. Army Quartermaster Foundation, http://old.quartermasterfoundation .org/LTG_Joseph_Laposata.htm.

27. Col. Kevin Kelley, letter to author, dated June 19, 2019. Laposata attended Indiana Teachers College, now Indiana University of Pennsylvania, while Pond had attended Georgia State. Pond once served as company commander for "The Old Guard" stationed near Arlington Cemetery. Pond's obituary can be found at: https://www.legacy.com/obituaries/starnewsonline/obituary .aspx?pid=167337787.

28. Christopher Ogden, *Life of the Party: The Biography of Pamela Digby Churchill Hayward Harriman* (Boston: Little, Brown, 1994); Frank Moore, e-mail to author, March 9, 2019.

29. Rolly Kidder and Frank Moore, e-mails to author, dated March 9, 2019; Mills, *Their Last Battle*, 77, 238n.

30. Woerner interview, February 28, 2019. The first president to not appoint a military chairman would be Donald J. Trump.

31. "President Clinton Appoints 9 Members to the American Battle Monuments Commission," White House press release, April 14, 1994. Guerra-Mondragon would be appointed as ambassador to Chile, then replaced by Ed Romero, who would be appointed ambassador to Spain.

32. Kidder, e-mail to author, March 9, 2019.

33. F. Haydn Williams Papers, Box 16, letters file, National Defense University Library Archives, Washington, D.C.

34. "President Announces Appointment of Fred F. Woerner and F. Haydn Williams as Members of the American Battle Monuments Commission," White House press release, May 27, 1994.

35. "Clinton Eulogizes Allies Who Died in Italy Campaign," *Los Angeles Times*, June 4, 1994.

36. Kidder narrative.

37. Williams Papers, Box 25, Normandy folder contains brochures about the cemetery.

38. Williams Papers, Box 25, Inspection Folder Suresnes American Military Cemetery and Memorial.

39. Woerner interview, February 28, 2019; Kelley letter, June 19, 2019.

40. Williams Papers, Box 25, Cemetery inspection folders.

41. Helen Fagin Papers, Box 1, National Defense University Library Archives, Washington, D.C.; Williams Papers, Box 16 has date lists of all of the meetings.
42. Williams Papers, Box 16, Appointment Letter from General Woerner dated October 24, 1994.
43. Pat Foote, e-mail to author, dated June 30, 2019. Admitted to Wake Forest in 1948, Foote spent her sophomore year attending George Washington University to save expenses.
44. Pat Foote, letter to author, dated June 19, 2019.

Chapter 2. Location! Location! Location!

1. "President Names Members of World War II Memorial Advisory Board," White House Press Release, dated September 29, 1994.
2. Todd S. Purdum, "Sarah McClendon, Reporter at White House, Dies at 92," *New York Times*, January 9, 2003.
3. "Helen Fagin, Visual History Biographic Profiles," *Echoes and Reflections: A Multimedia Curriculum on the Holocaust*, https://iwitness.usc.edu/sfi/Data /EchoesData/EchoesBios/PDF/Fagin.Helen.pdf. Fagin e-mail to author, July 2, 2019; Sidney Fagin's obituary is at https://www.legacy.com/obituaries /heraldtribune/obituary.aspx?pid=182190295.
4. "Helen Fagin, Visual History Biographic Profiles"; Fagin e-mail to author, July 2, 2019.
5. Maya Bell, "Holocaust Memorial Stirs Anger: Miami Beach Is a City Divided Over Monument," *Orlando Sentinel*, January 28, 1990.
6. The building was kiddingly dubbed "The Polish Pentagon" by its ABMC and Army Corps of Engineer inhabitants.
7. Fagin Papers, Box 2, Letter from Colonel Kelley dated October 17, 1994; Seating Chart and Agenda for MAB meeting of December 1, 1994; Kelley letter to author dated June 19, 2019.
8. Williams Papers, Box 16, Williams chronology for 1994–95.
9. Thomas B. Grooms, *World War II Memorial, Washington, D.C.* (Arlington, VA: American Battle Monuments Commission; Washington, D.C.: U.S. General Services Administration, 2004), 32, 34.
10. Fagin Papers, Box 2, Sarah McClendon report of January 20, 1994, to Memorial Advisory Board.

11. Rolland Kidder narrative provided to author, January 20, 2019.

12. Fagin Papers, Box 2, Letter from Helen Fagin to MAB dated February 9, 1994; Letter from Helen Fagin to Colonel Kelley dated February 9, 1994.

13. See Davis Buckley Architects and Planners, https://www.davisbuckley.com/; Williams Papers, Box 1, Parsons file, Letter from Williams to Parsons dated May 14, 2005.

14. Williams Papers, Box 1, Buckley Folder—Site Selection Report.

15. Fagin Papers, Box 2, Sarah McClendon memo to Peter Williams dated March 3, 1995. Williams noted that Fagin had preferred Site #1 but changed her vote to make the #4 choice unanimous.

16. "Holocaust Memorial Stirs Anger."

17. Williams Papers, Box 16, Williams chronology for 1994–95; Kidder e-mail to author dated July 25, 2019.

18. Mills, *Their Last Battle*, 83.

19. Williams Papers, Box 25, May 1995 trip.

20. Williams Papers, Box 1, Davis Buckley Folder, May 30, 1995 memo.

21. Williams Papers, Box 16, Williams chronology for 1994–95; Box 1, Parsons Folder, May 14, 2005, Letter from Williams to Parsons.

22. Mills, *Their Last Battle*, 84; Williams Papers, Box 1, Buckley Folder, Talking Points for June 20 NCMC meeting.

23. Fagin Papers, Box 2, Memo from the desk of Kevin Kelley to MAB Advisory Board Site Advice Committee.

24. Williams Papers, Box 16, Williams chronology for 1994–95.

25. Williams chronology for 1994–95.

26. Michael Kimmelman, "J. Carter Brown, 67, Is Dead; Transformed Museum World," *New York Times*, June 19, 2002.

27. Williams Papers, Box 4, Fact Sheet Dated November 1, 1995, Subj: Site for WWII Memorial.

28. J. Carter Brown Papers, John Hay Library, Brown University, Minutes of the Commission of Fine Arts Meeting dated July 27, 1995, 5.

29. Williams Papers, Box 1, Parsons Folder, Letter to John Parsons from Williams dated May 14, 2005.

30. Kidder e-mail to author dated July 25, 2019.

31. Williams Papers, Box 16, Williams chronology for 1994–95.

32. Fagin papers, Box 2, McClendon letter to MAB dated September 13, 1995.

33. Mills, *Their Last Battle*, 90; Williams Papers, Box 16, Williams chronology for 1994–95.

34. Rolland E. Kidder, *Backtracking in Brown Water: Retracing Life on Mekong Delta River Patrols* (iUniverse, 2014), back dustjacket biography. Kidder also conducted interviews with thirty-seven Jamestown area residents who served in World War II and published *A Hometown Went to War* (Chautauqua, NY: Sandy Bottom Press, 1996), which earned a Writer's Digest Best Life Stories Award.

35. Williams Papers, Box 1, Parsons Folder, Letter to John Parsons from Williams dated May 14, 2005; Mills, *Their Last Battle*, 91.

Chapter 3. The National Design Competition

1. Rolly Kidder narrative; Williams Papers, Box 4, Folder ABMC Commission Meetings 1995–96.

2. Mills, *Their Last Battle*, 4–5, 15–16; Williams Papers, Box 4, Folder ABMC Commission Meetings 1995–96. Haydn Williams was included in the ABMC contingent; Kelley letter to author dated June 19, 2019. Kelley claims credit for the idea of using soil from the cemeteries at a planning meeting with Lieutenant General Kicklighter in the Pentagon, following Kicklighter's suggestion of obtaining soil from various battlefields. Besides being considered more sacred, the soil from the cemeteries was also easier to collect.

3. Williams Papers, Box 4, Folder, ABMC Commission meetings 1995–96 Part II, November 1995 FACT SHEET; Mills, *Their Last Battle*, 164.

4. Ormie King, "Herrling: A Legend Who Rose to Major General," *The Citizen* (Auburn, NY), May 5, 2013; Herrling interview with author dated July 1, 2019.

5. Paul Cret Harbeson was the son of architect John F. Harbeson, who taught with the French-born Paul Cret at the University of Pennsylvania. Cret had earned ABMC contracts to build several memorials in Europe during the interwar years.

6. Fagin Papers, Box 2, November 9, ABMC WWII Memorial Design subcommittee agenda.

7. Fagin Papers. Box 2, Letter to MAB dated December 26, 1995; Rolly Kidder, "Haydn Williams and the Initial Design," point paper sent to author March 18, 2019.

8. Williams Papers, Box 4, First Draft: World War II Capital Campaign, November 1995.

9. Fagin Papers, Box 2, Helen Fagin Memo to MAB dated February 1, 1996.

10. Williams Papers, Box 4, Folder Commission Meetings 1995–96, Revised MOU of February 8, 1996.

11. Williams Papers, Box 4, Folder Commission Meetings 1995–96, Williams hand notes.

12. Williams hand notes.

13. Mills, *Their Last Battle*, 108.

14. Fagin Papers, Box 2, Col. Kelley March 28 Memo to MAB, Subj: Draft WWII Memorial Design Program.

15. Col. Kelley, March 28 Memo.

16. Mills, *Their Last Battle*, 109.

17. Paul D. Spreiregen, "A Democratic Approach For Our World War II Memorial," *Washington Post*, May 5, 1996.

18. Benjamin Forgey, "War Memorial Battle," *Washington Post*, May 21, 1996.

19. Mills, *Their Last Battle*, 112; "About the Prize," The Pritzker Prize, https://www.pritzkerprize.com/about.

20. Fagin Papers, Box 2, Bill Lacy letter to Haydn Williams dated June 6, 1996, attaching revised *Commerce Business Daily* announcement; Kidder, March 18, 2019 point paper.

21. "Changes To WWII Memorial Design Will Ensure Open and Fair Competition," GSA news release dated June 10, 1996.

22. Deborah K. Dietsch, "Memorial Madness," *Architecture* 85 (July 1996): 15.

23. St.Florian interview with author dated June 26, 2019.

24. Fagin Papers, Box 2, Helen Fagin Memo to Peter Wheeler dated July 5, 1996, Subj: July 1 meeting of the WWII Memorial Site and Design Committee.

25. Grooms, *World War II Memorial*, 58; Mills, *Their Last Battle*, 115.

26. Grooms, 42–43.

27. Grooms, 43; Willens/Siemer interview of Williams; Mills, *Their Last Battle*, 115.

28. Grooms, 43.

29. Benjamin Forgey, "Designs on History: Finalists Chosen for World War II Memorial," *Washington Post*, August 22, 1996.

30. Mills, *Their Last Battle*, 116.

31. Mills, 117.

32. Willens/Siemer interview of Williams.

33. Mills, *Their Last Battle*, 116.

34. Grooms, *World War II Memorial*, 43, 59; Mills, *Their Last Battle*, 118.

35. Williams Papers, Box 4, ABMC/MAB meeting FACT SHEET: ABMC Office Space.

36. Dietsch, "Memorial Madness," 15; Roger Lewis, "Proposed World War II Memorial Site is Land Worth Fighting Over," *Washington Post*, August 17, 1996.

37. Haydn Williams, "The Right Place for a Memorial," *Washington Post*, September 29, 1996.

38. Fagin Papers, Box 1, Bill Lacy letter to Helen Fagin.

39. Mills, *Their Last Battle*, 142.

40. See: Weiss/Manfredi, http://www.weissmanfredi.com/.

41. See: Rafael Viñoly Architects, https://www.vinoly.com/.

42. See: CallisonRTKL, https://www.callisonrtkl.com/.

43. Ambroziak would go on to become an associate professor of architecture at the University of Tennessee at Knoxville.

44. See: Balmori Associates Landscape and Urban Design, http://www.balmori.com/.

45. St.Florian interview with author dated June 26, 2019.

46. An architect with Skidmore, Owings & Merrill, Childs had been involved in the redevelopment of the Pennsylvania Avenue corridor in Washington, D.C., and later would design the new World Trade Center post–September 11, 2001.

47. Grooms, *World War II Memorial*, 56; Mills, *Their Last Battle*, 132.

48. Williams Papers, Box 1, David Childs Folder, David Childs Letter to Haydn Williams dated October 31, 1996.

49. Fagin Papers, Box 2, Memo from Helen Fagin to MAB dated November 7, 1996.

Chapter 4. The Joy of Victory and the Agony of . . .

1. St.Florian interview. St.Florian actually had been studying at a gymnasium in Salzburg and had been sent home following a bombing. To help him continue his education, his mother arranged for him to attend a girls' academy that had been relocated to a hotel in his village.

2. Mills, *Their Last Battle*, 138–141; Grooms, *World War II Memorial*, 106.

3. St.Florian interview.

4. Rolland Kidder, "Success and then Retreat," point paper dated March 25, 2019.

5. Mills *Their Last Battle*, 134.

6. Benjamin Forgey, "World War II Memorial Design Unveiled," *Washington Post*, January 18, 1997; Robert Gee, "Clinton to Unveil Design Today for WW II Memorial," *Baltimore Sun*, January 17, 1997.

7. Kidder point paper sent to author.

8. Williams Papers, Box 4, ABMC Commission Analysis of Direct Mail, Stephan Winehall & Associates, Inc.

9. Williams Papers, Box 4, ABMC-MAB folder, Williams January 1997 memo.

10. Fagin Papers, Box 2, Woerner Letter to Wheeler dated February 28, 1997.

11. Fagin Papers, Box 2, Fagin memorandum to MAB dated February 19, 1997; Mills, *Their Last Battle*, 144.

12. Fagin Papers, Box 2, Fagin memorandum to MAB dated March 26, 1997; Mills, *Their Last Battle*, 94–95.

13. Williams Papers, Box 1, Williams letter to Senator Inouye dated April 7, 1997.

14. Fagin Papers, Box 1, May 1, 1997, Site and Design Meeting notes; Herrling interview by author July 1, 2019; *Battle of Normandy Foundation: Uncertainties Surround Its Future Viability*, GAO Report B-259129 dated November 4, 1994.

15. Mills, *Their Last Battle*, 146.

16. Fagin Papers, Box 2, Mangis letter to Fagin and Fagin response dated April 18, 1997.

17. Fagin Papers, Box 2, May 12, 1997, Site and Design Meeting notes.

18. Williams Papers, Box 4, Fact Sheet dated April 29, 1997, Subject: World War II Memorial Capital Campaign.

19. Fagin Papers, Box 2, Fagin memorandum to MAB on June 30, 1997, SDC meeting; Williams folder Box 2, Editorials Folder; Brown Papers, Brown Letter to Ms. Lindroth and Mr. Newick dated May 19, 1997.

20. Mills, Their Last Battle, 148–49.

21. Fagin Papers, Box 2, Wheeler memorandum to MAB dated July 8, 1997. St.Florian admitted later that the fifteen-foot pit in the original concept denied visitors the important element of seeing the Lincoln Memorial.

22. St.Florian interview.

23. Mills, *Their Last Battle*, 147; Minutes of the Commission of Fine Arts Meeting of July 24, 1997; Roberta Hershenson, "The Fight for the World War II Memorial," *New York Times*, July 27, 1997; Associated Press, "World War II Memorial Site is Backed but the Design is Not," *New York Times*, July 25, 1997.

Chapter 5. The Comeback

1. "Designers Go Back to Drawing Board on Proposed World War II Memorial," *Baltimore Sun*, August 12, 1997.

2. Kidder, "Success and then Retreat"; Roberta Hershenson, "The Fight for the World War II Memorial," *New York Times*, July 27, 1997; Mills, *Their Last Battle*, 146.

3. Kidder point paper.

4. Mills, *Their Last Battle*, 148.

5. Fagin Papers, Box 2, Fagin memorandum to Herrling and Williams.

6. Williams Papers, Box 4, Folder ABMC Commission Meetings, memorandum dated September 3, 1997, Subj: Contract with Burson-Marsteller, and memorandum dated September 3, 1997, Subj: Public Service Announcement Program.

7. Mills, *Their Last Battle*, 165. Rolland Kidder credits John Herrling for actually recruiting Smith.

8. Williams Papers, Box 4, Folder ABMC Commission Meetings, memorandum dated September 4, 1997, Subj: Gifts from Foreign donors; and memorandum dated September 4, 1997, Subj: Solicitation of ATF companies.

9. Fagin Papers, Box 2, Kidder memorandum to Williams and Fagin dated September 20, 1997.

10. Williams Papers, Box 1, Fagin Folder, Fagin memorandum to Williams and Kidder dated September 22, 1997.

11. Mills, *Their Last Battle*, 149; Fagin Papers, Box 1, Notes for MAB meeting of November 10, 1997.

12. Fagin Papers, Box 1, Woerner letter to Fagin dated December 10, 1997.

13. Williams Papers, Box 1, Appelbaum folder, December 19 proposal from Ralph Appelbaum Associates.

14. Williams Papers, Box 1, Appelbaum folder, Williams notes of Herrling call: Subj: Schlossberg and Appelbaum.

15. Mills, *Their Last Battle*, 139; St.Florian interview. St.Florian recalled that Adele Chatfield-Taylor, CEO of the American Academy in Rome, graciously hosted the group at her New York headquarters.

16. Fagin Papers, Box 1, 1998 folder, SDC and Content Subcommittee Meeting of February 23 notes.

17. Williams Papers, Box 1, Bloomberg folder, Record of conversation with John Parsons, March 3, 1998.

18. Fagin Papers, Box 1, 1998 folder, Williams letter to Thurmond; Thurmond letter to Dole dated March 25, 1998.

19. Linda Wheeler, "World War II Memorial—A Lower Profile," *Washington Post*, May 13, 1998.

20. Fagin Papers, Box 1, 1998 folder, Statement of Senator Kerrey, dated May 20, 1998.

21. Mills, *Their Last Battle*, 151; Minutes of the Commission of Fine Arts, dated May 21, 1998.

22. Williams Papers, Box 1, David Childs folder, Childs letter to Williams, dated June 3, 1998.

Chapter 6. Tom Hanks Arrives on the Scene

1. Williams Papers, Box 2, Williams letter to Shelly, dated August 23, 1999.

2. Herrling interview with author, dated July 1, 2019; Woerner phone call with author, dated June 12, 2019. Because of the sensitivity of filming a movie on the burial grounds of American war dead, Herrling insisted on reviewing the movie script before allowing Steven Spielberg to film on location. Mike Conley drafted the letter to Hanks.

3. Mike Conley e-mail to author dated July 16, 2019.

4. Williams Papers, Box 4, ABMC Commission Meeting folder, ABMC ExComm Meeting of December 3, 1999, PowerPoint overview. Fayos letter courtesy of Mike Conley.

5. Conley interview with author, dated July 15, 2019.

Chapter 7. The Evolving Design

1. Williams Papers, Box 1, Helen Fagin Folder, Fagin memorandums to Williams dated July 15 and 17, 1998; Williams memorandum to Fagin dated July 27, 1998.

2. Fagin Papers, Box 2, SDC Memorandum to St.Florian dated August 27, 1998.

3. Fagin Papers, Box 2, Minutes of September 16 World War II Memorial Site and Design Committee; St.Florian interview with author dated June 26, 2019.

4. Fagin Papers Box 2, Draft minutes of October 15, 1998, SDC meeting.

5. Fagin Papers, Box 2, Feldman letter to St.Florian dated October 8, 1998.

6. Fagin Papers, Box 2, Draft minutes of October 15, 1998 SDC meeting.

7. Williams Papers, Box 2, Schlossberg Inc. Folder: October 15 Content development Study p. 38.

8. Fagin Papers, Box 2, Fagin letter to Williams dated October 26, 1998.

9. Fagin Papers, Box 1, Minutes of the Joint ABMC/MAB meeting at the Arlington Hyatt, November 1998.

10. St.Florian interview; Grooms, *World War II Memorial*, 71. A side chapel in the basilica of Santa Maria in Trastevere features four cherubs holding a wreath; Williams, Box 1, Helen Fagin Folder, Minutes of the December 19, 1998, SDC meeting.

11. Fagin Papers, Box 2, Williams Memorandum to St.Florian dated January 29, 1999.

12. St.Florian interview.

13. Fagin Papers, Box 2, Fagin letter to Williams dated February 2, 1999.

14. Fagin Papers, Box 2, Minutes of the February 8, 1999, SDC meeting.

15. James S. Russell, "Art and Politics Vie in a Battle to Honor A Monumental War," *New York Times*, April 4, 1999.

16. Williams Papers, Box 4, ABMC Commissioner Meeting Info Paper Subject: WWII PR update dated April 6, 1999.

17. Williams Papers, Box 4, ABMC Commissioner Meeting Info Paper Subject: WWII Memorial Project Budget Status.

18. Frank Moore, phone interview by author dated July 10, 1999; Frank Moore, exit interview with Dr. Thomas Soapes, dated December 17, 1980, Carter Presidential Library and Museum, https://www.jimmycarterlibrary.gov/assets/documents/oral_histories/exit_interviews/Moore_Frank.pdf.

19. Commission of Fine Arts Minutes for May 20, 1999.

Chapter 8. Completing the Design

1. Williams Papers, Box 1, Helen Fagin folder, Fagin letter to Williams dated August 31, 1999.

2. St.Florian interview.

3. Fagin Papers, Box 2, Striner to Feldman letter dated August 6, 1999; Feldman to Striner letter dated August 10, 1999; Striner letter to Feldman dated August 20, 1999.

4. Fagin Papers, Box 2, Brown letter to Boasberg dated October 8, 1999; Williams letter to Boasberg dated October 22, 1999; Linda Wheeler, "Monumental Proposal: Plan Would Ban New Memorials in Most of Mall," *Washington Post*, September 9, 1999, B1, B7.

5. Fagin Papers, Box 2, Williams memorandum of October 27, 1999; Mills, *Their Last Battle*, 157–58.

6. Williams Papers, Box 1, Hart letter to Williams dated November 9, 1999; Williams letter to Hart dated November 11, 1999; Hart letter to Williams dated November 12, 1999.

7. Rolland Kidder interview with Friedrich St.Florian dated April 11, 2019.

8. Fagin Papers, Box 2, Notes of December 6, 1999, SDC meeting; Moore e-mail to author dated July 25, 2019; Kidder e-mail to author dated July 27, 2019.

9. Fagin Papers, Box 1, Dillon e-mail to Fagin dated January 11, 2000.

10. Fagin Papers, Box 2, Williams memorandum to St.Florian dated February 3, 2000.

11. Grooms, *World War II Memorial*, 88.

12. St.Florian interview. Rolland Kidder credits Ray Kaskey with the wreath concept.

13. Williams Papers, Box 1, John Hart folder, Hart letter to Williams dated January 26, 2000.

14. Williams Papers, Box 1, John Hart folder, Hart letter to Williams dated February 18, 2000.

15. Kidder e-mail to author dated April 29, 2019.

16. Williams Papers, Box 4, ABMC Commissioners Meetings 1997–2001 folder, February 18, 2000, Information Paper.

17. Williams Papers, Box 1, Ambrose folder, Williams notes of February 24, 2000 meeting.

18. Williams Papers, Box 1, Ambrose folder, Williams letter to Ambrose dated March 7, 2000; Ambrose letter to Williams dated March 13, 2000.

19. Christopher Shea, "Brawl on the Mall," *Preservation News*, January–February 2001, 43.

20. Fagin Papers, Box 1, Williams memorandum to St.Florian dated April 12, 2000, Subj: SDC Working Group Meeting April 2000; Grooms, *World War II Memorial*, 102.

21. Williams Papers, Box 1, Senator Inouye folder, Williams letter to Inouye dated April 14, 2000.

22. Fagin Papers, Box 1, Williams memorandum to St.Florian dated May 8, Subject: SDC Working Group meeting of May 5–6; Grooms, *World War II Memorial*, 107.

23. Fagin Papers, Box 1, Williams memorandum to St.Florian dated May 26, Subject: SDC Working Group meeting of May 20.

24. Williams Papers, Box 1, Inouye folder, Williams letter to Reid dated May 23, 2000.

25. Brown Papers, Brown letter to Ada Louise Huxtable dated July 28, 1997; Fagin Papers, Box 2, Linda Wheeler, "Dole Raps Critics of Memorial as 'Late,'" *Washington Post*, June 7, 2000.

26. Williams Papers, Box 4, ABMC Commissioners Meeting 1997–2001 folder, June 27–28, 2000 meeting notes and edited scripts of the Childs presentation.

27. Fagin Papers, Box 1, Herrling letter to ABMC and MAB dated July 31, 2000.

Chapter 9. The Groundbreaking

1. Fagin Papers, Box 1, Herrling letter to MAB dated July 31, 2000.

2. Mills, *Their Last Battle*, 179–80; Kidder e-mail to author dated May 3, 2019. Kidder believes that if Williams had been there, his presence could have won the day.

3. Williams Papers, Box 2, Critical Article folder; Williams draft response to *Wall Street Journal*.

4. Mills, *Their Last Battle*, 178–79.

5. Fagin Papers, Box 1, Fagin letter to editor, *New York Times*, dated September 26, 2000.

6. Jim Garamone, "Groundbreaking Ceremony Held for World War II Memorial," *Armed Forces Press Service*, November 14, 2000. Mills, *Their Last Battle*, 17.

7. Williams Papers, Box 6, Groundbreaking folder, Williams speech; Mills, *Their Last Battle*, 183.

8. Williams Papers, Box 6, Groundbreaking folder, Williams speech.

9. Garamone, "Groundbreaking Ceremony Held for World War II Memorial."

10. Mills, *Their Last Battle*, 178; Williams Papers, Box 2, Responses to Critical Articles folder, Foote and Fisher e-mail exchange of November 14, 2000.

11. Williams Papers, Box 6, Personal papers folder, Woerner letter to Bush, undated.

12. Williams Papers, Box 6, Personal papers folder, Pond letter to P. X. Kelley dated December 6, 2000.

13. Kidder letter to author dated June 20, 2019; Woerner phone conversation with author dated June 12, 2019.

Chapter 10. On to the Dedication

1. Fagin Papers, Box 1, Foote letter to Brown dated December 19, 2000; Brown letter to Foote dated December 28, 2000.

2. Kidder e-mail to author dated May 13, 2019.

3. Williams Papers, Box 1, Campbell file.

4. Mills, *Their Last Battle*, 184–85.

5. Williams Papers, Box 1, Campbell file.

6. Mills, *Their Last Battle*, 185–86.

7. Mills, 186–87.

8. Benjamin Forgey, "An Overdue Honor for WWII Veterans Once Again Is Unjustly in the Line of Fire," *Washington Post*, May 5, 2001.

9. Mills, *Their Last Battle*, 194–95.

10. Williams Papers, Box 2, Inscriptions folder, Williams memorandum dated October 5, 2001; Fagin Papers, Box 1, Kelley letter to Williams dated November 1, 2001.

11. Williams Papers, Box 6, Personal folder, Herrling letter to Williams dated November 9, 2001; Fagin Papers, Box 1, Williams facsimile to Working Group dated November 9 for forthcoming meeting.

12. Mills, *Their Last Battle*, 201.

13. Williams Papers, Box 2, Inscriptions folder, Williams report to Kelley dated November 26, 2001.

14. Williams Papers, Box 2, Inscriptions folder, Williams memorandum for the Record.

15. Williams Papers, Box 2, Inscriptions folder, Williams memorandum to Fagin dated December 12, 2001; Fagin comments to author, e-mail dated June 13, 2019.

16. St.Florian interview.

17. Fagin Papers, Box 1, Fagin letter to Herrling dated April 23, 2002.

18. Fagin Papers, Box 1, Fagin memorandum to Williams dated June 7, 2002; Fagin note to Williams dated July 1, 2002.

19. Foote letter to author dated June 19, 2019.

20. Fagin Papers, Box 2, Kelley update memorandum to ABMC and MAB; Grooms, *World War II Memorial*, 91, 113.

21. Fagin Papers, Box 1, Kelley announcement of November 11, 2002; Williams Papers, Box 6, Personal papers folder, Wheeler letter to Williams dated March 25, 2002.

22. Williams Papers, Box 1, St.Florian folder, St.Florian letter to Williams dated June 27, 2003; St.Florian interview.

23. Grooms, *World War II Memorial*, 94, 108.

24. Stephen R. Brown, *Jewel of the Mall: World War II Memorial* (self-published, 2011), 56, 84–88.

25. Fagin Papers, Box 1, Folder C-1, Foote Memorandum for the Record dated March 2, 2004 on March 1 meeting; Kidder e-mail, May 13, 2019.

26. Williams Papers, Box 1, General Herrling folder, Herrling letter to Williams dated April 30, 2004.

Epilogue

1. The author interviewed former Chief of Naval Operations Adm. James Holloway and Senator John W. Warner during a Library of Congress oral history presentation.

2. Fagin e-mail to author dated May 20, 2019.

3. Michael Janofsky, "Veterans Gather to Dedicate World War II Memorial," *New York Times*, May 30, 2004; Video footage of the National Cathedral service and the dedication is archived on C-Span.

4. Fagin e-mail to author dated May 27, 2019.

5. Williams Papers, Box 1, David Childs folder, Williams letter to Childs dated August 10, 2005; Childs letter to Williams dated September 12, 2005; Margaret F. Williams obituary, *San Francisco Chronicle*, December 2–4, 2005.

6. Fagin Papers, Box 1, folder C1, Memorandum for the Record dated October 23, 2006.

7. Williams Papers, Box 6, WWII Memorial October 2006 folder, Minutes of the Old Working Group, Washington, D.C., October 29–31, 2006. A Trust for the National Mall would be formed, see: https://www.nationalmall.org/.

8. Williams' complete statement can be found at: http://www.wwiimemorialfriends .org/10th-anniversary-commemoration/. He paid special tributes to Kaptur, St.Florian, and Brown.

9. Video of reading provided to author by the Friends of the National World War II Memorial.

INDEX

fundraising, 78; groundbreaking ceremony and, 133; Herrling's MAB appointment and, 54; invited to chair ABMC, 17–18; joint campaign and policy committee and, 57; MAB and, 48; relieved as ABMC chairman, 136; Site and Design Committee and, xxi, 21; on Williams, 137

World War II, xv, xvi–xvii, 14, 15

World War II 50th Anniversary Commemorative Coins Act (1992), xviii

World War II Memorial: construction contracts for, 143; dedication, events marking, 148, 153–57; dedication, public visits prior to, 151; ground-breaking ceremony, 133–35; groups visiting, 161–62; legislation support-ing, xvii–xix; local opposition to, xxiii–xxiv; newsletters, 65; site dedication for, 52–53; St.Florian scaled down design, 78–79; Williams' on Sicily-Rome American Cemetery and, 18–19. *See also* Friends of the World War II Memorial; Site and Design Committee

World War II Memorial Advisory Board (MAB): accepting St.Florian design, 72; first, composition of, 24–30; first meeting of, 30–31; groundbreaking ceremony and, 133–35; joint campaign and policy committee with ABMC, 57; meeting, Korean War Memorial dedication and, 43; Public Relations and Fundraising Committee, 56; reunion luncheon, 162–63; revised memorandum of understanding with ABMC and, 49; site selection subcommittees, 32–36. *See also* Old Working Group; Site and Design Committee

World War II Memorial Completion Act, 112

World War II Memorial Design Consultants, 143

Wulff, Bernard J., 69

WWII Memorial Capital Campaign playbook, 56

Yardley, Jonathan, 127

Zumwalt, Elmo R., Jr., 2

ABOUT THE AUTHOR

David F. Winkler is the 2020–21 Smithsonian Air and Space Museum Charles Lindbergh Fellow in Aerospace History following a year as the U.S. Naval Academy Class of 1957 Chair of Naval Heritage. Having served two decades as the Naval Historical Foundation staff historian, Winkler holds a PhD from American University, an MA from Washington University, and a BA from Penn State. He is a retired Navy commander, having served twenty-eight years on active duty and in the Reserve.